FROM LOSS
TO LEGACY

FROM LOSS TO LEGACY

HOW A FASHION BUSINESS ROSE FROM HAITI'S RUBBLE

JULIE COLOMBINO-BILLINGHAM

BOLD STORY PRESS

CHEVY CHASE, MARYLAND

Bold Story Press, Chevy Chase, MD 20815
www.boldstorypress.com

Copyright © November 2025 by Julie Colombino-Billingham

All rights reserved. No part of this book may be reproduced or used in any manner without written permission of the copyright owner except for the use of quotations in a book review. Requests for permission or further information should be submitted through info@boldstorypress.com.

First edition: November 2025
Library of Congress Control Number: 2025918313
ISBN: 978-1-954805-97-2 (hardcover)
ISBN: 978-1-954805-76-7 (paperback)
ISBN: 978-1-954805-77-4 (e-book)

Cover design by Amelia Baerlein,
inspired by Emmanuelle Alexander
Cover photo from iStock.com/Claudiad
Interior design by KP Books

Printed in the United States of America
10 9 8 7 6 5 4 3 2 1

○

This book is dedicated to my families:
the one I was born into in the United States,
and the ones I've been privileged to find
in the United Kingdom and Haiti.

Thank you for teaching me
determination, pride, and resilience,
especially my husband, Billy.

Thank you for allowing me
to love so deeply and be loved.
I am humbled to have been
so blessed in my life.

○

CONTENTS

Foreword ix
Preface xi

CHAPTER 1 Nineteen Degrees North of the Equator 1
CHAPTER 2 Setting Trends 25
CHAPTER 3 I Don't Want Water 39
CHAPTER 4 REBUILD globally 59
CHAPTER 5 Jolina 77
CHAPTER 6 Where It All Started 99
CHAPTER 7 Finding My Place 109
CHAPTER 8 Love in a Hopeless Place 125
CHAPTER 9 Family Affair 151
CHAPTER 10 New Beginnings 167
CHAPTER 11 Deux Mains 179
CHAPTER 12 Fashion Forward 197
CHAPTER 13 Faith or Fashion? 215
CHAPTER 14 Remember, Rise, and Rebuild 227
CHAPTER 15 Motherhood 241
CHAPTER 16 Walk a Mile in Our Shoes 255
CHAPTER 17 The Soul of Money 275

Acknowledgments 291
About the Author 293
About Bold Story Press 295

CUBA

HAITI

DOMINICAN REPUBLIC

Port-au-Prince

PUERTO RICO

CARIBBEAN SEA

FOREWORD

○

As a military man for more than twenty-seven years, I have seen great tragedy and suffering, but none greater than that caused by the earthquake of 2010 in Haiti. In this memoir Julie tells step by step the true stories of suffering, the survivors' resilience and courage, and the novel solutions found to problems when greater powers had given up. She shares the pain and also the humor of her truly remarkable journey that continues even today. You can feel the emotion and smell the reality through every chapter as if it's your own experience. This book shows that miracles can be achieved against all odds, captured for all of us to benefit from in our ever-changing, complex world.

Julie's depth of knowledge is second to none. She earned it not just from her degrees, but more importantly from her being on the ground days after the earthquake, living and learning through one of the worst natural disasters ever known. This book could almost be the training bible for dealing with catastrophic situations by relying on experience, honesty, integrity, and lessons learned. There is no substitute for real experience.

Mark Billy Billingham, MBE

PREFACE

○

Ten million people call Haiti home. I am privileged to know a few dozen Haitians, whose lives have been forever intertwined with mine. The words on these pages are their stories, which overflow with a strength that comes from facing devastation in the most intimate way. I've had more than a decade to process them, as well as my own experience with the earthquake, and I still find myself coming back to the moment when I knew my life would change forever, the night I felt an unexplainable but undeniable urgency to go to Haiti. I lay awake, restless, trying to make sense of this pull toward an island I knew almost nothing about. Why did this conviction grip me so completely, refusing to let go? Even now, it's hard to describe, only that it was powerful enough to override logic and leave me certain I had to go. By morning, exhausted from a sleepless night and unsettled by the intensity of it all, I carried on with the day as if it were any other.

National Public Radio murmured in the background as I made the two-mile commute to the Heart of Florida United Way, where I worked as the volunteer manager. However, that

| 1600–1700s | 1791 | 1804 | 1825 | 1915 | 1934 |

- **1600–1700s**: The western portion of Hispaniola, Saint Domingue, is colonized by the French
- **1791**: Slaves in Saint Domingue, soon to be known as Haiti, begin their fight for freedom
- **1804**: Haiti wins its independence in the first successful slave rebellion. Other world powers with slave-owning interests refuse to recognize Haiti as the first free Black republic.
- **1825**: French navy ships sail to Haiti and demand a ransom. Haiti agrees to pay 150M francs for winning its freedom
- **1915**: US seizes control of Haiti and declares martial law for the next 17 years
- **1934**: American troops leave Haiti, but it is crippled economically from these experiences

morning the news wasn't ordinary. It carried a weight that pressed into my chest, each word heavier than the last. Fifteen hours earlier, the earth had shaken so violently that Haiti's capital city of Port-au-Prince had crumbled to the ground. Those thirty-five seconds of terror and destruction maimed the country and stole countless lives. The voices of the radio correspondents trembled as they reported the magnitude of the catastrophe. The death toll climbed by the second, and the number of missing seemed infinite. I gripped the steering wheel tighter, trying to understand the enormity of the disaster unfolding just a few hundred miles away, and completely overwhelmed, now understanding why I felt God's nudge toward Haiti the night before.

The earthquake remains one of the greatest natural disasters to have occurred in my lifetime, and it compelled me to travel to its shattered shores. What I witnessed in my

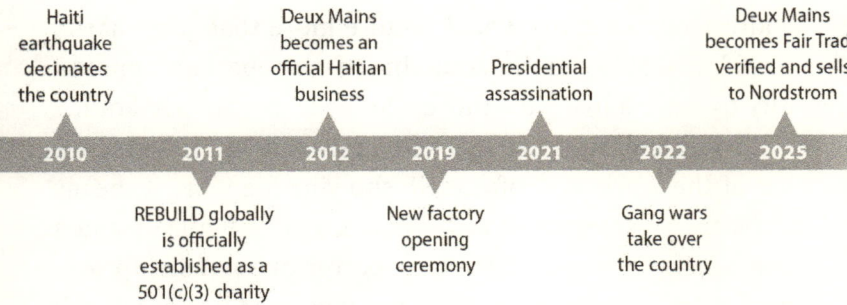

first twenty-four hours stole a layer of innocence I can never reclaim. But this book isn't just about that horrific day. It's about a turning point that reshaped my understanding of poverty and led me on a path of rebuilding. When I first arrived in Haiti, I was consumed by grief. I mourned the death of thousands, sitting with mothers who had lost their children, and children who had lost their mothers. I witnessed unimaginable pain, but as I spent more time in Haiti, my eyes opened to another kind of loss, a quiet, unspoken one that blanketed the landscape: the loss of economic opportunity and dignity.

I saw it everywhere. People who wanted to work and provide for their loved ones went hungry, not because they lacked the will, but because they lacked the opportunity. Families remained homeless because there was no path forward. I was drowning in the poverty that plagued this developing island nation. It was an epidemic, a force as destructive as any natural disaster, silently killing hope, crushing spirits, and destroying lives. Over time, I came to understand that addressing this crisis would require more than just charity or aid. It would require something far deeper: an opportunity to make a living for those who had been stripped of it.

Living and working in Haiti reshaped my understanding of the world and of myself, showing me what it means to be truly accountable as a woman, a global citizen, and a consumer. I discovered the true power of partnership over pity. It wasn't easy to set aside preconceived notions, but it was transformative, allowing me to approach the developing world in a completely different way. From Loss to Legacy is a tribute to those who have survived unimaginable tragedy, and who amid their own suffering still find it within themselves to educate others, making this also the story of my own transformation from disaster responder to job creation activist.

Haiti is the birthplace of our charity, REBUILD globally, and our business, Deux Mains ("two hands"). It is where we discovered that education and fashion could converge to create a system that empowers people while honoring their talent and indigenous wisdom. Together, we confirmed that fashion can be free-thinking, fair, and world-changing. In doing so, we found a way to change our own life stories and will perhaps inspire others to change theirs too. I hope this book might open your heart to experiencing tragedy through a new lens, to appreciating the unshakable determination of the Haitian people, and to understanding the beauty and complexity of Haiti's land

and complicated past. The country's struggles extend far beyond recovering from the earthquake, as its people have endured centuries of suffering, first imposed by outsiders and later from within.

As this book goes to print in 2025, Haiti continues to face extraordinary challenges. The ongoing political instability, escalating gang violence, and humanitarian crisis have forced many Haitians to flee their homes, while those who remain face severe food insecurity and limited access to basic services. Yet even in these darkest hours, the fortitude I've witnessed over the past fifteen years endures. Our team at Deux Mains continues their work despite overwhelming obstacles, embodying the unbreakable spirit I describe throughout these pages. While the situation may seem hopeless from the outside, I've seen firsthand how Haitians refuse to surrender their dignity or abandon hope for their beloved country. Their determination strengthens my conviction that economic empowerment remains a vital path forward. Now more than ever, Haiti needs partners, not saviors—people willing to listen, learn, and stand alongside Haitians as they build their own solutions. It is my sincere hope that sharing these stories will inspire meaningful solidarity with Haiti during this critical time, honoring both its profound struggles and its immeasurable strength.

CHAPTER 1

NINETEEN DEGREES NORTH OF THE EQUATOR

Every shadow—no matter how deep—
is threatened by morning light.
Unknown

○

January 12, 2010, 4:53 p.m.

The building began to shake violently. Everyone started screaming and crying and running in all directions. There were hundreds of merchants and shoppers at the market. It was madness. My stall was placed by the front door, and when the wall started to shake, I ran for my life. When I was outside of the building, I didn't stop running. I ran for the next two hours to get home to my family. On the streets, people everywhere were bleeding, crying, and screaming. When I finally got to my neighborhood, it was dark. Those who survived were putting the children who were alive under a tree, and the women who were not severely injured were trying to get them to go to sleep.

I found my two daughters under that tree. I then found my husband, who was pulling bodies from the rubble with some of the other men. My family slept in the field that night. I remember we had nothing, and it was so cold.

The next morning there were still children in the streets crying. My best friend Denise and I realized many of these homeless children had lost their parents in the earthquake.

The UN and the Red Cross gave us a tarp and some food, so we took the orphaned children with us to Denise's yard, because she had a big space. We made the tent out of the materials provided by the relief agencies. I would go out and ask people and organizations for help as we started with ten children, and within months it grew to thirty-six. We needed to find a way to make this sustainable for these children.

Jolina Desroches

On January 25, 2010, I boarded a plane from Miami, Florida, to join hundreds of other volunteers heading to Haiti. It had been just thirteen days since one of the deadliest earthquakes recorded in the Western Hemisphere had decimated the country. I knew I needed to go, but no amount of resolve could prepare me for the devastation I was about to encounter. There wasn't a certificate, a college program, or a reality show that could prepare a human being to work in the landscape of post-earthquake Haiti. The experience would change my world view and challenge everything I believed.

Before the earthquake, in what I now call my pre-Haiti life, I was practicing a life of minimalism. I had spent a few months in South Africa in the early 2000s, living with a host family that didn't have much by material standards but whose members shared what they had with generosity and joy. Their way of life, rich in tradition and connection, left an indelible mark on me. When I returned to the States, I resolved to stay connected to that experience. I traded in my TV for stacks of books, prepared simple meals to share with friends, and donated most of my clothes to charity. I made a conscious effort to buy less and opted for secondhand items when possible, in an effort to stop contributing to all the waste in the world. My life became quieter, more intentional, and I connected to my local community in a more significant way. With this lifestyle came a tendency to stay a step removed from the constant noise of breaking news, so I often heard about world events later than most. The Haiti earthquake was no exception. It wasn't until the morning after the quake that the news report on the radio pierced through my routine. An earthquake had struck Haiti, and the destruction was unimaginable.

Hearing about it was one thing, but seeing it was another. When I arrived at my office and stepped into the reception area, the television was on, broadcasting images of Port-au-Prince in ruins. Buildings lay flattened, survivors wandered in shock, children screaming in the streets and frantic rescuers clawing through debris. It was unbearable to see, and impossible to look away from.

The weight of the moment settled over me and I knew it would mark a new beginning. It was as if the life I had carefully curated, the simple quiet life I had been living, had been upended in that instant. I knew this tragedy wasn't something

I could observe from a distance. Being a part of the earthquake recovery was the reason I felt so drawn to Haiti.

Acting on instinct I bypassed my cubicle and walked right into Lori's office without knocking. Desperate to get my supervisor's attention I sharply asked, "What are we doing to help Haiti?" Lori, taken aback by my abruptness, looked up from her desk to tell me that no plans had yet been made. She waved toward the door and went back to the papers she was signing.

Without thinking I blurted out, "Since I'm a certified disaster responder, I would like to take my two-week vacation to volunteer for the Haiti response effort." I was so curt; I barely recognized the person speaking. My disaster-response training prepared me to take action during moments like this, but this time was very different. My entire being felt propelled toward Haiti. I couldn't ignore the feeling in my gut and I was blinded by my determination to get there.

I was convinced the United Way would support my conviction, so I began wrapping up my most pressing tasks to prepare for the time off, when Lori stepped into my cubicle to deliver the news: my vacation request had been denied. I paused for a moment, considering what she had said, and then I thanked her for the opportunity to work at United Way and respectfully resigned from my job. I think we were equally stunned, but this wasn't a decision based on logic or practicality. I had felt a summons that defied everything, and it seemed as if there was no other option for me. Lori walked away and I began packing up my personal belongings. I was very fortunate that within the hour, my bosses at United Way reversed their decision and approved my two-week vacation, allowing me to deploy to Haiti without losing my job. As I slowly unpacked my things and set them back on my desk, I felt a deep sense of gratitude.

In the days that followed, I made the necessary arrangements to travel from Miami to Haiti. I reached out to everyone I knew, asking for donations of tents, money, and packaged food. Soon my living room was filled with supplies, everything from bottled water to shampoo. Even my dentist pitched in, donating hundreds of toothbrushes and tubes of toothpaste, while friends in the medical field sent bandages and first-aid kits. I didn't know what I was going to do with it all; I just believed I needed it.

As word spread about my impending deployment, I was connected with a local network of Haitian churches and businesses in my community that were organizing their own efforts to help. That is how I met Jean and Frank, two men from Orlando who were equally determined to get to Haiti. Jean's family lived in Port-au-Prince, and he was desperate to know of their situation. Being around Jean, I began to see how deeply personal this disaster was for so many people. It wasn't just a tragedy on the news; it was affecting people I knew, and whom I now cared about.

After the earthquake and for the weeks that followed, no one could purchase airline tickets to Haiti. However, Vision Airways was offering free flights for volunteers. There were no baggage limitations, no weight restrictions; it was the wild west of disaster response. After the three of us felt we had enough supplies in hand, we made the three-hour drive from Orlando to Miami in the middle of the night to catch one of the volunteer flights. Miami Airport was in disarray when we arrived. Hundreds of people were sleeping on the floor and dozens more were pacing the corridors, all eager to help in any way they could.

Given the enormous demand for seats and the difficulty of landing a plane safely in Haiti, flights were scarce, and we waited several days for our turn to board one. The 700-mile flight from Miami to Port-au-Prince would normally take just under two hours, but our journey stretched across the day and into the night. Our landing attempts were aborted several times due to aftershocks, forcing the 747 with hundreds of anxious volunteers to circle above Haiti for hours. The absence of a ground crew to assist our landing only delayed us further. Most of the passengers were from the University of Miami Hospital, medical professionals charged with the most difficult task of caring for the wounded, crushed, and dying. It was agonizing to be flying above such destruction when we had lifesaving equipment and doctors on board. My heart burned as I imagined what it was like for the people on the ground watching us circle above them for so long.

It was after 9 p.m. when we touched down on what used to be the landing strip of Haiti's main international airport, now no longer recognizable. There was no terminal building, no customs office, no procedure to follow. The raw truth of the loss and destruction hit me. As soon as the doors of our plane opened, a rush of exhausted and injured relief workers surged on to secure seats for their return flight to the United States. They had been in Haiti since the quake hit. Covered in dust and blood, wearing facemasks and backpacks, they frantically pushed and shoved past us as we tried

January 25, 2010, Port-au-Prince, Haiti. Destruction of homes in a neighborhood just miles from the international airport.

to exit. I could feel their desperation to escape the hell we had just landed in, and my heart quailed at the thought of what they had suffered. But they were the lucky ones. They were leaving. I was about to enter a space where millions of Haitians had endured the same suffering and had no possibility of escape. This was their home and there was no leaving for them. With this realization my courage returned. Grabbing my backpack, I fought my way off the plane.

Moments later I was standing in the thick dust and rubble of Haiti's capital city. The acrid stench of death filled the air, and piercing cries of grief overwhelmed my senses. As I was trying to get my bearings, four white trucks sped alongside the belly of the plane. Men jumped from the trucks and rushed into the baggage compartment, rapidly unloading everything into the beds of these pickups. Without warning, the trucks then drove off, disappearing into the sea of people gathered around us. All that remained was me—a scared volunteer in a strange country, stripped of all my gear except a notebook, $600 in cash, and my passport, all in a backpack slung over my shoulder. No toothbrush. No change of clothes. Nothing of real value. The gravity of the situation was becoming very apparent. What had I gotten myself into?

I stood, trying to gather my thoughts, but the noise of chaos and desperation was deafening. I looked around, trying to make sense of the scene. There was nothing but crowds of people in the midst of an unholy struggle, their faces marked by exhaustion and fear. I had come to help, but now, with everything I thought I'd bring to the table taken away from me, I felt naked and powerless in a land of devastation.

It wasn't until weeks later that I learned the men in the white trucks weren't just random scavengers. The plane we'd flown in on was considered a "medical flight," and the men had been told to retrieve all the baggage and surgeons on it for the medical clinic that was being constructed down the road. The situation was critical and every second mattered. I also learned later that the airport wasn't just a place for commercial air transport anymore; it had been turned into a logistics center for the US Army and an array of nonprofits. This decimated place where we'd landed was the hub of the relief efforts.

Deciding to deploy to Haiti with Jean and Frank made the familiar weight of my disaster-zone experience feel suddenly hollow. Without an organization behind me, the safety net, the structure, the clear directives were not there this time. Without this official reinforcement I felt exposed and vulnerable in a way I hadn't anticipated. During the chaos of exiting the plane and the distraction of losing my bags, I had also lost sight of Jean and Frank. Panic surged through me as I spun around, scanning the havoc that surrounded me, desperate to find them. Just as I was about to lose hope, I spotted them standing near the tail of the plane. I ran toward them, relieved to be back by their side. Our reunion was a brief moment of stability before we merged into the desperate crowds to search for Jean's family.

When we finally found them, Jean's older brother ushered us into an old Ford truck that looked like it had barely survived the quake itself. I climbed into the open space where a car door had once been and sat close to the driver, bracing myself for what was to come. The next hour was like something out of a horror movie, a surreal, slow-motion descent into the heart of despair in which I was a strange combination of spectator and actor. Smoke hung heavy in the air, carrying with it the faint scent of burning wood and the unmistakable metallic tang of blood. I locked eyes with survivors whose hollow gazes told stories of unimaginable loss. Children were everywhere. Some silently clung to their mothers; others sat on the remnants of walls, screaming into the abyss, while some simply roamed the streets. But the streets were no longer recognizable roadways; they were nothing more than the ruins and remains of a city.

Our driver zigged and zagged through the rubble and the crowds. I didn't understand the language and there was no way I could have conceived the depth of loss, yet at this moment it engulfed me. We drove only a few miles, but it was late into the night by the time we arrived at Jean's parents', and I almost didn't recognize the building as a house. Most of the walls were cracked or crumbled, the structure barely standing. His parents were waiting for us outside, their faces lined with exhaustion. Without hesitation they embraced us, offering us newcomers what little comfort they could. They led us into what was left of their home and offered us water from a gallon bucket sitting on the floor of their mangled kitchen. Most of the family were still sleeping outside, their fear of collapsing walls keeping them away from buildings at night. But for the comfort of their foreign guests, they had prepared the only room left unscathed for us to sleep in. A few mattresses were placed on the ground next to the door, with sheets and pillows smelling faintly of the smoke that lingered everywhere.

The family's fears of aftershocks were not unwarranted. The initial 7.0 magnitude earthquake had been followed by relentless aftershocks measuring 4.5 or greater. Tremors continued to batter the area throughout the following weeks, and Jean's family warned us to be ready to run outside if another one hit. We felt the earth softly trembling beneath us that night, but worse was the sound of women praying and singing through the darkness, their voices mingling with the endless howls of dogs. It was a chorus of anguish mixed with hope that hung in the air. As the night pressed on, my throat began to ache from the smoke and dust that was impossible to escape.

The destruction was absolute, and no home, school, or business had been safe from the earthquake's fury. The disaster had reduced more than 300,000 buildings to nothing but rubble. Roads were cracked open like fault lines, swallowing cars and blocking movement. More than 60% of government and administrative buildings were destroyed, including the Presidential Palace, the National Assembly, and the United Nations headquarters. The human toll was staggering. An estimated 230,000 people had been killed, 300,000 more were injured, and more than 1.5 million were left homeless. Entire families had just vanished beneath the debris, and the streets became graveyards of desperation as people searched frantically for loved ones. Haiti's fragile economy and daily life had been brought to a standstill; with 80% of the population already living in poverty, a massive humanitarian crisis lay ahead. I was now at the center of a genuine catastrophe, destruction deeper and wider than the human mind could process in one night. It was impossible to sleep.

Morning brought no reprieve. Before the first light of dawn we were ready to walk, through air thick with ash and crumbled cement, to work at the provisional medical clinic in the mountains near Jean's home. The tattered tarp that outlined the clinic area was held together by rocks and rusted rebar. Holes in the plastic rustled in the wind, tearing bigger with every gust that came. Lines of people seeking help stretched beyond the hill where the clinic stood. Most hospitals in the city had been rendered unusable, leaving places like this the only option for the injured. With no medical background, I was given the simple task of irrigating and bandaging wounds. But it quickly became apparent that no task was simple in these conditions.

The first patient's leg had been shredded by falling debris. The gash was deep and infected, the edges swollen and red. My hands trembled as I reached for the irrigation supplies, only to realize there weren't any. No sterile syringes. No proper medical tools. Just a Neti Pot, the kind you'd use to clear nasal passages. I stared at it in disbelief, but there was no time to hesitate. The man's eyes pleaded with me, his lips pressed tight to stifle his groans. I filled the pot with saline and tilted it over his leg. The liquid trickled into the wound, flushing out dirt, shards of concrete, and pus. His wound was so severe that under normal circumstances it would have required surgery. He flinched, but he didn't make a sound. I fought back the lump rising in my throat as I grabbed a roll of gauze and wrapped his leg.

The day blurred into a relentless cycle of wounds, infections, and tears. Some patients were stoic, their pain controlled by years of hard living. Others screamed, their cries piercing the tarp walls and echoing in the pit of my stomach. I moved from one to the next, rinsing gaping holes with the Neti Pot, wrapping broken skin with bandages that ran out too quickly. As the sun dipped behind the mountains, I bandaged the last patient of the day, a girl no older than six with a jagged cut running down her arm. She didn't cry or even flinch as I tied the gauze around her wound. When I finished, she looked up at me and whispered, "*Mèsi*" (thank you). I turned away, unable to face her bravery.

The following day I was assigned to hand out expired Tylenol to those who needed morphine injections for pain. It felt cruel to offer such meager relief. Our situation was bleak, but I had no choice other than to adapt, though every act of triage weighed heavy on my soul. Late that afternoon, a young boy with asthma was carried into the clinic. Dust from the collapsed buildings had infiltrated his lungs, and his wheezing was sharp and haunting. I watched, helpless, as clinicians tried to treat him on a pile of rubble, but all their attempts seemed to be in vain. His breaths became slower, weaker, until the sound of his struggle faded into silence. Agony was no longer an abstract concept or a story. It had a face now, that of a boy with wide, terrified eyes and lungs that couldn't find air. I was different after that day.

We left the clinic just before dark, and I was trying to comprehend why all this had happened. Why were people forced to experience such misery? I felt a deep anger at the lack of support to help people. The poverty that had existed before the earthquake so exacerbated the situation that it nearly paralyzed any effort we made. Nonexistent building codes had left thousands of people trapped and dying beneath broken building foundations. Children were already malnourished, so they didn't have the strength to fight for their lives. The electric power grid, which had been unreliable before the disaster, failed completely, and we lost communication lines. Even if our phones had been working, there was no one to call for help, because everyone needed help. We had nothing to operate with and no infrastructure on which to rely. The morgues were quickly reaching capacity, and corpses were being left in the streets. The poverty all around us was making a horrific situation completely intolerable.

I had traveled to other impoverished places, but I had never seen suffering like this. In those dismal hours, I began to hate not just nature but also, those responsible for this neglect. For three days my anger burned as I went back to that clinic and continued to be crippled by our lack of resources. I felt useless and incompetent in the tragedy's vastness. Every day I was at the clinic, I felt myself falling deeper into a tunnel of despair. I couldn't wrap my head around cleaning wounds that would ultimately lead to someone's death. I couldn't live with knowing that people were coming to me for help, and in some cases I was only prolonging their suffering. I had no real solutions and no business working in medical care. I was angry with God for what was happening and for putting me in this situation.

As I poured peroxide onto four-year-old Stevenson's toe, his bloody little toenail fell off. Even then, he never took his eyes off me. He had more deep wounds than any child should ever have, but he didn't seem bothered by them or the fact that we had run out of soap to clean them properly. He just sat stoically across from me and allowed me to apply Neosporin to his open flesh. As I looked back into his eyes, I knew I had a choice to make: fall deeper into despair and become a burden myself, or find a way to do things differently. In that moment I felt a sense of hope creep into my brain. If I could let go of everything I knew and treat every circumstance with respect for the survivors, considering what their lives had been like before this disaster, maybe it would be possible for my work here to achieve something of significance, and maybe something extraordinary could happen in my life too.

The latter part of my day was spent silent and watchful, looking for some sort of sign to tell me what to do next, but all I saw were the injured survivors, the hot and frustrated volunteers, and the merciless dust that circulated with every gust of wind. I knew somehow, however, the surge of peace I had felt earlier would be a huge part of my future if I were brave enough to change. After a lot of deliberation and prayer, I mustered all the strength God granted me, and on the following morning I decided to leave the medical clinic and my only friends in Haiti. Frank, Jean, and his family begged me not to leave them. They were worried about my safety and shocked that I would go off on my own, but once again, despite having even less certainty this time around, I knew I needed to follow my gut.

Walking away from the clinic with rubble and swirls of dust at my feet, I hitched a ride with a man in a red Toyota Rav4 that had taken a severe beating from the earthquake. I could tell from his kindness and exhaustion that he was working tirelessly to help his country recover. Together we went back down the mountain, saying little due to my inability to speak the local language of Creole. The man helped me make my way back to the airport landing strip where I had originally arrived. For some reason this was the place I felt I needed to be, and I was somehow able to communicate that to him. Moments later, I was walking into a large tent camp for relief workers.

There, I was taken in by the Volunteer Ministers, the Scientology group known as the VMs or "yellow shirts," for the bright yellow t-shirts they all wore every day. With more than 25 years of disaster response experience, the VMs had quickly taken a leadership position within the array of nonprofits and other responders, and I could tell they were respected. Despite all the continued confusion and madness of the situation, they were well organized and seemed to have an endless stream of volunteers. For weeks I worked alongside them, watching the way they put systems in place to distribute the new information that was coming in every hour and to group volunteers based on skill sets, and each day I was learning new lessons that empowered me to get things done more efficiently.

It had now been nearly a month since the earthquake hit and people were still working in a frenzy, but in an attempt to bring order, the efforts were at least divided among sectors—health and hygiene, food distribution, rubble clearing, and so on. Each sector had an organizational structure and one of the most valuable skills I learned from the VMs was how to get in contact with the highest-ranking person in each sector, ensure they knew who we were, and get on the lists to have access to the most up-to-date information.

The VMs were also geared up to respond to the needs of the relief workers. I was working on autopilot and had no idea how much strength and mental capacity were being drained by each moment. I was filthy and exhausted. I forgot to eat and use the toilet, unless I was suffering from one of many bouts of diarrhea from the unsanitary conditions. There was no time to rest, no way of bathing, no dignified privacy.

Even though I was functioning at my maximum capacity, I could never do enough or feel satisfaction about what I had accomplished in a day. The VMs knew that the feeling of inadequacy is common to disaster responders, especially in these sorts of extreme conditions, and they were prepared to care for us. There was a tent where we could get MREs (military ration emergency meals) or granola bars, and a medical tent I visited frequently, given that injury and illness became a part of daily life. My approved vacation from United Way had long run out, but time didn't exist in this place and I didn't care anyway.

I found comfort and friendship with two women in the camp, Kim and Malia. Their impact on my life has been profound, and they became the catalysts for my long-term work in Haiti. I knew from the beginning we three would be a force to be reckoned with. We bonded quickly over our anger at the bureaucracy and the slow pace of the distribution efforts. It was infuriating, and we were eager to insert ourselves into the daily bottlenecks of aid distribution, believing we could do it better. We understood that the lack of local leadership made it complicated to distribute aid well. Many of the people with local knowledge who would normally organize these activities had died in the earthquake, and their passing left a huge void. Water purification tanks, food, and medications were rotting on the provisional runway in Port-au-Prince, with no plan or labor force to get them into the community. By following the relief agencies' rules, we ended up being a part of this broken system.

As time went on, however, we found ways to rebel, not just against the slow processes set up by the relief agencies, but against the havoc of the entire system that was being built. We created our own path. We were gritty and cared little about the red tape the large organizations had to work through, so we were able to act. We developed a system for taking unclaimed supplies from the airport and distributing them to the surrounding community. Kim, Malia, and I built a small team of some of the most knowledgeable people on the ground, and before we knew it, we had organized a system where a group of local people delivered goods to those most in need. We were fortunate that one of our new friends, James, owned a car that hadn't been destroyed in the earthquake. As part of our morning routine, we visited the airstrip like scavengers, taking anything we could find and fit into his car. After filling every vacant inch of the backseat with supplies, we would set off to the most remote places we could find. Given the waste and disorganization around us, no one challenged our methods or questioned our actions.

In the early 2000s Kim and Malia had both lived in Florida and attended the same church. With their common love of travel and culture, they became fast friends. A few years later Malia took a real estate job in Hawaii. She loved the island life and held onto her career for a while following the 2008 financial crisis, but after a year of struggling she decided to move back home to Clearwater to be closer to her mother and sister. She and Kim hadn't seen each other in years, but their friendship took off right where they had left it. Before they knew it, they were dancing at nightclubs and drinking coffee on the strip as if no time had passed. Before the earthquake they had made big plans. Kim was working as a freelance artist in Tampa, and with her husband deployed to Afghanistan, she and Malia saw a perfect opportunity to pursue a long-held dream to backpack through Europe.

Days before they were to leave on their big European adventure, the earthquake destroyed Haiti. Malia, having served with the VMs during 9/11, was not a novice at disaster relief and knew she could be an asset. She didn't think twice about giving up her vacation plans, nor did she have to work hard to convince Kim to come along. Kim agreed they would deploy to Haiti and serve under the VMs to help Haiti recover. Rising to leadership positions on the ground within the organization, Kim and Malia saw how they complemented each other, not just as friends but as disaster responders. Malia was intent on getting things done quickly, and Kim had the diplomacy needed to allow them to work thoughtfully in their response efforts.

With my eagerness for action I seemed to fit right in with their working style, and they quickly welcomed me into their group. We found comfort working and living together, relying on each other's strengths. Malia was quick to make friends, and she soon met a man named Reggie who, like most Haitian people, was doing his best to help anyone he could. Reggie was so impressed by the way we were getting things done that he gave us his truck to use, so we could make bigger deliveries and get to parts of the city we couldn't access with James's car. With wheels of our own, we had the independence to make things happen even quicker. We somehow also wiggled our way into the most important logistics meetings happening at the United Nations Logistics Base. Log Base, as it was known, was the nucleus of the response coordination efforts, and at the time we didn't know how valuable to our future in Haiti the relationships we were forming there would be.

By now I had been in Haiti more than a month. The days blurred together in a haze of heat, dust, and relentless work. Even if I'd wanted to leave, the few flights available were prioritized for emergency evacuations, leaving volunteers like me with no way back to the States. But I wasn't ready to go, not yet. There was too much to do, too much unfinished. I convinced myself that staying was not just an option but my duty, and for a while I was at peace with it. I was able to Skype with my bosses back in Orlando, and although the internet connection crackled and froze, I managed to explain the situation. I asked for more time, a chance to extend my vacation and stay in Haiti. They agreed, offering their blessing. With the threat of losing my job gone, relief washed over me. But just as quickly as I'd made the decision to stay, my body announced other plans.

It started suddenly, an ache that spread like wildfire, followed by waves of nausea. Within hours I was violently ill. My strength, which had carried me through so many days, crumbled. I spent the next 48 hours in my tent, curled up next to two buckets—one for each end of my body, both betraying me with relentless ferocity. Not accustomed to the illnesses of this land, by nightfall I could barely move. Every muscle ached, and the oppressive heat felt unbearable. I lay there, weak and trembling, realizing for the first time that I might not be able to stay. The goal to which I had committed myself now seemed to be slipping through my fingers, and I felt utterly helpless.

I had met Sam, a woman from California, a few weeks earlier, and like me, she was now battling a debilitating stomach virus and knew she needed medical treatment. With international flights grounded, she was determined to find a way out. Sam had a knack for logistics, and like so many other VMs, she knew where to get reliable information. One day she heard a rumor.

"There's a small plane," she told me. "It's leaving Port-au-Prince for the Dominican Republic." With little earthquake damage in the DR, flights to the United States were running normally, so if we could manage to get to the other side of the island safely, we could then take another flight back to the United States. The Dominican Republic shares the island of Hispaniola with Haiti and is bordered by the Atlantic Ocean to the north and the Caribbean Sea to the south. Just east lies Puerto Rico across the Mona Passage, and to the west the waters open toward Cuba and Jamaica. From above, the island looks like a bridge between worlds. One landmass, two countries, each with its own story.

I'd run out of money by then, my resources drained along with my strength. When I told Sam I was broke, I expected her to hesitate. After all, she barely knew me. But she didn't think twice and bought me a ticket for the flight to the Dominican Republic. A few hours later, with Sam beside me, gratitude swirled with guilt as I buckled in, clutching my stomach. Our plane lifted out of the bedlam of Port-au-Prince and into the air, leaving Kim and Malia behind.

The short flight was unpleasant, as I was still tethered to a bucket toilet like a lifeline. The mere thought of being without one for even a few minutes sent waves of anxiety through me. As the Gulfstream aircraft began its descent, I gripped the armrest and squeezed my eyes shut, praying I could hold myself together for just a few more seconds. My stomach churned as the plane touched down, and I knew I was on borrowed time. The moment we were cleared to deplane, I bolted—no polite smiles, no second glances. I tore through the terminal like a woman possessed, my desperation creating a scene that turned heads. Security officers shouted after me in a language I didn't understand, their commands only adding to my panic. When they stopped me, I clutched my stomach, tears spilling down my face. Words failed me, but my body told the story. After a tense pause, one officer seemed to understand. He gestured hurriedly, and I darted toward the nearest bathroom, too frazzled to say thank you.

I thrust open the stall door, barely making it in time. As I leaned over the toilet, my relief was short-lived. My passport slipped from my trembling hand and landed in the bowl. I froze, staring at it in disbelief, the scene so vile I couldn't bring myself to react right away. The tears came again, this time from pure humiliation. I fished the document out, my hands shaking, the stench making my stomach churn all over again. When I stumbled back to customs, clutching my soaked passport like a badge of shame, I couldn't even meet the officer's gaze.

But even in that moment of utter degradation, something deeper stirred within me. The past seven weeks had felt like the longest of my life, but the whirlwind of emotions wasn't pushing me away from Haiti. Rather, as clearly as the exhaustion that weighed on my body, it was anchoring me deeper. I knew with absolute certainty that my work in Haiti wasn't done. Not even close.

CHAPTER 2

SETTING TRENDS

A society grows great when old men plant trees whose shade they know they shall never sit in.
Greek Proverb

○

Realizing we were too ill to travel back to the States immediately, Sam and I spent the next few days in a little cobblestone hotel in the Dominican Republic, where I drifted in and out of sleep, more from pure exhaustion than from the virus that still wracked my body. I was indebted to Sam for getting me out of Haiti and bringing me to this little sanctuary with a bed, clean sheets, and a bathroom that didn't require a bucket. Lying there, I came to realize that my mind needed to process what I had experienced just as much as my body needed to rest.

The contrast between Haiti and the Dominican Republic was staggering. Even though the DR covers about two-thirds of the island of Hispaniola, it was far from the epicenter of the earthquake. Here the streets were untouched, the buildings intact, the air buzzing with life instead of desperation.

The guilt of escaping while so many couldn't lingered in my chest, even as my body began to recover. But the calmness of the DR also gave me time to think about my next step. It allowed me to process what Haiti was supposed to mean for my future and the work I wanted to do there. It was in that little hotel room that the solution crystallized: I needed to establish my own charity to create the change I envisioned.

When I made it back to Orlando a few days later, my fiancé Noah was waiting, his face a mix of relief and concern as I walked toward him. He listened in disbelief to every heartbreaking detail I sputtered out. It must have sounded crazy. My stories of events in Haiti were unbelievable, my experiences too much to comprehend. There were things I couldn't bring myself to tell him. Some were too raw to share. Instead, I focused on what I thought he could handle, leaving the rest locked inside. By the time I finished, though, it wasn't my stories that shook him the most; it was the decision I had already made. Sitting there, I told him with quiet certainty, "Noah, I'm going back to start my own charity." This wasn't just a passing thought or an emotional impulse; it was a conviction, an unshakable truth I had come to realize. My life in Haiti was just beginning.

Noah's shoulders slumped as he took it in. He wasn't angry, not exactly, but I could see the frustration in his eyes. "You just got out of there alive," he said, his voice tight. "And now you're telling me you're going back?" I didn't have an answer that would satisfy him. All I knew was that Haiti had changed me, and there was no going back to the life I had lived before. And though I didn't yet know how, I was certain Haiti would change my future too.

Noah didn't say much about my plans over the weekend. He was mostly calm, though I caught a flicker of something in his eyes, disbelief perhaps? I suspect he thought this was just an impulsive, emotionally driven idea that would fizzle out before it truly began. The following Monday morning, however, I walked into the United Way office with my resignation letter neatly folded in my bag, my heart pounding in rhythm with the heels of my shoes against the tiled floor. It wasn't a decision I had made lightly, but it felt right, like the first step of a journey I was finally ready to take. My two weeks' notice would give me time to train my replacement, leave on good terms, and mentally prepare for the leap I was about to make, a leap both figurative and literal. I imagined most of my colleagues thought I had temporarily lost my mind, though they were too polite to say so outright and were outwardly supportive. A few, however, knew better. They understood my knack for veering off the beaten path.

One of my colleagues, Brittany, even smirked knowingly and said, "This is so you." And it was. She knew the stories and even experienced a bit of my rebel spirit in our time working together. Years earlier, in 2004, I'd nearly lost my job at the Community Service Center (CSC), a nonprofit in Orlando focused on ending homelessness, for what my boss called "reckless behavior." The CSC headquarters wasn't much to look at, a small, scrappy-looking building tucked into a corner of downtown Orlando. But it was filled with people who cared deeply about the mission. I fit in ideologically, but I wasn't content to simply serve our clients from a distance, and my methods often raised eyebrows.

One afternoon on my way to get lunch at a sports bar, I saw an unhoused man who looked hungry. I was intrigued by him and wanted to get to know him, so I invited him to eat with me. Just as we started to scan the menu options in the bar, the manager appeared at our table. His eyes wandered between me and my new companion, his face a mix of disgust and impatience.

"You'll have to leave," he said firmly, motioning toward the door. I protested, but the manager wouldn't budge. I was shocked at the way we were treated and will never forget the way the manager looked at my companion. It was the day I decided I needed to understand why, in a country with so many programs to support struggling people, so many still fell through the cracks. That resolve led me to pursue a new opportunity to manage a community-building program for vulnerable people in Orlando. This program was taking place housing complex called Maxwell Terrace, a converted Motel 6 turned into low-income housing.

The residents were a patchwork of humanity, many sleeping indoors for the first time in years. Some were transitioning out of homelessness, others battling HIV/AIDS, and still others working through mental health issues or addiction. Seniors with nowhere else to go filled the remaining rooms. With all these different personalities in such tight living quarters, tensions ran high. The county decided a project was needed to bring these people together and create a sense of belonging, and I saw an opportunity to learn. Maxwell Terrace became my classroom, its residents my teachers. I spent my days navigating their challenges, celebrating their small victories, and trying to piece together the puzzle of systemic poverty.

Maxwell Terrace was supposed to be a step up from the streets, but it felt more like a forgotten corner of life. Roaches scuttled across cracked walls, the exteriors were rotting, and the air smelled faintly of mildew and despair. Then there was Mr. Quinton, the unofficial ruler of the neighborhood, a gang member whose presence made it clear that power here was not in the hands of any authority figure but him. Walking through those halls, I knew I was a novice at understanding the lives of the poor. I had grown up in a middle-class family, cocooned in economic privilege, and my inability to comprehend how people survived here stymied me. I knew I couldn't truly help if I didn't understand their situations in depth. So I formed a drastic plan to learn what the residents at Maxwell Terrace experienced. I decided instead of just creating a community-building project, I would move into the complex and live among them.

The idea stubbornly took hold, but before I could bring it to my boss, I confided in Bridget and Sonya, two of my closest friends and colleagues. The moment the words left my mouth, they exchanged a look of alarm.

"That's . . . noble," said Bridget slowly, "but it's not exactly safe."

Sonya nodded. "There's got to be a better way, J."

And then, as if their minds were in sync, they began to hatch a plan. "What if," Bridget began, leaning forward, "we collaborate with someone at UCF [University of Central Florida], maybe the College of Social Work?"

Sonya jumped in, her voice rising with excitement. "We could write a report! Use part of the funding from the community-building program to document the truth about Maxwell Terrace. We'd have data, research. It'd be something the city couldn't ignore."

Their enthusiasm was contagious, and the plan began to take shape in my mind. Working with a professor from UCF, we would shine a light on the dire conditions Maxwell Terrace residents faced, conditions that local nonprofits and city officials seemed content to sweep under the rug. Somewhere, someone had to be responsible for coordinating efforts to address these living conditions. But from where we stood, it seemed like resources were being spent on optics rather than solutions. Money that could have transformed lives was being used as a Band-Aid, covering up wounds instead of healing them. We didn't have all the answers, but we were determined to change that. Together we would expose the truth, force people to confront it, and push for real, lasting change.

Bridget, Sonya, and I had first crossed paths at UCF. Even though we were driven by the same passions and working toward the same degree (a master's in nonprofit management), the differences between us were striking. Bridget and I, in particular, were polar opposites. She commanded attention without even trying. In the classroom she always claimed the front row, dressed in her little gray blazer, fingers flying over her mini laptop. Back then laptops in classrooms were rare, but there she was, diligently typing every word our professor uttered. She had the answer to every question, always prepared, always precise. I, on the other hand, as a double major in dance and nonprofit management, barely made it to class on time most days, fresh from sneaking in an extra ballet lesson. I'd slink into the back row in my sweatpants, listening intently, but only jotting down scattered notes when something piqued my interest.

Despite working at the United Way while tackling her master's degree, Bridget exuded a quiet confidence I admired. I wanted to land an internship with United Way, one of the largest and most respected charities in the country, so I reached out to her, hoping for advice. Happy to help, Bridget met me at a wine bar near her office downtown a few weeks later. What I thought would be a quick exchange of pointers turned into hours of conversation over glasses of wine. We quickly bonded over our frustrations with the status quo in nonprofit management. Both of us were brimming with ideas about how to challenge the broken systems we saw, even if our approaches couldn't have been more different.

Bridget was methodical and possessed a kind of energy I found captivating. She even had a knack for creating inventive meals, like salads made from outdated cans of vegetables "borrowed" from the food pantry at work. She called it resourcefulness; I called it genius. In turn, Bridget discovered that I was an innovator, someone willing to bend the rules if it meant getting things done. My conviction was both a strength and a liability, but she made a choice early on: if she wanted to be in my life, she would have to support me, even when she didn't fully understand or agree with my methods. That mutual respect and understanding became the foundation of our friendship. It was a partnership built on shared ideals, complementary strengths, and an unshakable belief in one another. It was no surprise to me that years later Bridget came to serve as the board chair of the charity we eventually formed in Haiti.

Sonya, the youngest of us, joined the team as a summer intern at CSC. Her energy and wit were electric, keeping us on our toes with every conversation. One sharp comment from her clever tongue could silence a room for hours. Sonya had a way of cutting through pretense and getting straight to the heart of an issue, and she never hesitated to speak her mind. At the time I was far meeker, and I admired her courage in openly discussing even the most controversial topics without fear. Our differences made us a powerful trio: Bridget's systematic brilliance, Sonya's fearless outspokenness, and my rebellious determination to push boundaries. We were young professionally, just peaking in our revolutionary spirits, and we spent our formative years together working on many community-building projects in Orlando.

I trusted their opinions, and they convinced me that my plan to move into Maxwell Terrace was taking it too far. I soon got on board with their idea to collaborate with professors at UCF, and it worked beautifully. The partnership led to the creation of what we called The Listening Project, which was as simple as it sounded: the process was listening to people in the community. For months we immersed ourselves at Maxwell Terrace, meeting with residents, absorbing their resilience, their heartbreaks, and their dreams. We even enlisted other UCF students to join us in conducting interviews. Those months were powerful for me. I learned that listening, not just hearing but truly listening, was one of the most powerful tools for creating change. It was a lesson I would carry with me well beyond Orlando, all the way to Haiti and throughout my work in communities around the world.

At the end of our work, we published a formal report titled "The Maxwell Terrace Listening Project." This document shared the residents' stories in their own words, highlighting how they ended up in these circumstances and what kept them bound there. Our report didn't pull any punches. We named the nonprofits that had failed Maxwell Terrace, exposing the inefficiencies and waste that plagued our sector. We wanted to put faces to the individuals most affected by these failures, to show the human cost of a system designed to mask problems rather than solve them. The consequences of our honesty were swift and brutal. Our grant funding was pulled, and we were reprimanded by our employers in various ways. I may have been considered an activist to some, but to others in Orlando's nonprofit circles my name became synonymous with troublemaking. I had no regrets, though. I knew we had done the right thing, even if it came at a cost.

As I waved my final goodbye to my colleagues at the United Way, I stood at another crossroads. But, this time the path ahead felt clearer. Maxwell Terrace had planted a seed I hadn't recognized before, a glimpse of what was possible when conventional charity fell short. Now, however, I didn't want to simply document those shortcomings; I was ready to act. I had the degree, the tools, and even some familiarity with failure. The stage was set, though it would be far from Orlando, right in the heart of Haiti, where my unconventional path would find its true destination. The charity I wanted to build would fundamentally reimagine the approach, building from the ground up with dignity, listening at the core of every step I took.

In addition to leaving my job, I was eager to tie up all the other loose ends in the States and get back to Haiti as quickly as possible. A few friends in Orlando who supported my decision helped me make the final arrangements. My friend Kari arranged a garage sale for me to sell the meager household items I owned, while I put my house on the market. It was 2010 and Florida was in the throes of a severe housing crisis, chalking up the nation's third-highest decline in home prices. It was hardly a seller's market, but in the end, I was able to walk away with $7,000 from the sale of my home and the savings I had acquired. It was all the cash I had to take back to Haiti with me, and I naively believed it would last a while.

I was confident about my decision to work in Haiti, but I couldn't stomach the thought of doing all of it on my own. Kim and Malia had become my anchors, and I wanted to continue working with them. My exit from Haiti three weeks earlier had been abrupt, and it had left me with no way of contacting them. All I knew about these women was their first and last names and that they were both from Tampa, but that was enough. My obsession with finding them led me to a phone number for Mary, Malia's mother. As soon as I found it I dialed, my heart pounding, and when she answered, the words poured out.

"Hi, Mary, you don't know me, but I met your daughter Malia at the VM camp in Haiti," I began, my voice trembling with emotion. "She kept me going during the hardest days. I want to go back to Haiti, and I need to find her and Kim. Can you please help me get a message to them?" Mary listened patiently as I spilled my guts, recounting every detail of my experience. I was so desperate, so earnest. When she could finally respond she said,

"They'll be on a flight back to Tampa in four days."

I nearly dropped the phone in relief and anticipation. I was already daydreaming about our reunion when Mary's voice cut through my thoughts.

"Would you like to pick them up from the airport?" she asked.

"Yes!" I blurted out. For the first time in weeks, I felt hope rising in my chest. In just a few days we would be together again, ready to figure out the next chapter, together.

The following Wednesday, Noah and I made the drive from Orlando to Tampa International Airport. We were about to pick up my friends and I was going to ask them to do something monumental: pack up their lives, move to Haiti, and start a nonprofit organization with me. To set the tone, we made a stop at a 7-11 along the way. Nostalgia guided my choice as I grabbed a six-pack of Colt 45, one of the only beers we could get our hands on in Haiti when the supply of Haitian-made Prestige ran out. As we waited for their plane to land, Noah tried to temper my anticipation.

"Remember how you felt when you first got back to the States," he said gently, his voice laced with concern. "You were completely overwhelmed. You cried so hard you could barely breathe." I knew he was preparing me for the possibility that Kim and Malia might find the idea of going back to Haiti crazy. He didn't think that in my still-fragile state I would be able to handle the rejection. I wasn't worried, though. He couldn't possibly understand the sort of bond we had formed in such a short time, inexplicable to someone who hadn't been there. That is one of the beautiful things about disaster relief work: there is no hiding from who you are. When you are in a pit of complete despair, the things that matter to you become clear very fast, and relationships quickly take on intense new meaning.

As Noah and I were talking, I saw two filthy, exhausted women walk out of the terminal. Initially confused by my presence, they stopped dead in their tracks. Then Malia screamed "JUUUULEESSS?" and we ran with open arms to reconnect.

We had so much to say we couldn't stop speaking over each other. Immediately, our little trio was reestablished. As we cracked open the Colt 45s in the airport parking lot, I couldn't wait. I told them that after everything we had seen and learned, I was determined to start my own charity and I wanted them by my side. I had my master's degree in nonprofit management, and both Malia and Kim were strong leaders and loved Haiti, so what could go wrong with this plan? I had prepared an elaborate pitch on why we should embark on this journey together, but persuasion proved unnecessary. Within minutes they were convinced by my simple argument: having witnessed firsthand what other organizations were doing wrong, we could create something better, a nonprofit that listened to the people of Haiti and worked closely alongside them, allowing their expertise to guide us in the reconstruction efforts.

Noah and I spent the next few nights in Tampa with my friends while we strategized our plans to get back to Haiti. We would put every effort and every penny we had into the recovery effort and return to the devastated little nation independent of any aid group. We would defy the systems we felt were broken and do our best to help this country to which we had all felt so drawn. Kim's husband was still deployed to Afghanistan, Malia was in a career transition, and with Noah's blessing, we were all free to return to the disaster zone.

It took a few more weeks for me to arrange everything for our move to Haiti, and as I cleared the last things from my house before the sale was final, I realized I was now houseless in the United States. I sat on the front porch of what used to be my home as it hit me what I had done. I clung to my faith, however, and the fear slowly dwindled. Soon I would be back in the ruins and rubble, and any problems I had here would be nothing compared to the situation people in Haiti faced.

CHAPTER 3

I DON'T WANT WATER

I can be changed by what happens to me.
But I refuse to be reduced by it.
Maya Angelou

○

We had temporarily escaped the harsh reality of Port-au-Prince while in Florida, but the mayhem enveloped us the moment Kim, Malia, and I returned. It was late March, and although aid efforts had been going on for months, our return felt different. On our own, with no organization backing us, our situation was more intense this time—no constraints, no one to answer to, but no one to take care of us either. Without the framework for our charity established, we threw ourselves into whatever relief work we could find. The workload was insurmountable, and the environment was unforgiving. We poured sweat from the extreme daytime heat, nearly fainting from dehydration, while helping to construct temporary shelters. Clouds of dust and dirt followed us around, sticking to our skin as we worked to coordinate food drops for orphanages. The nights were cold and wet, with torrential downpours that seemed to laugh at us in their fury. The weather was wearing down both our shelter and our resolve.

Every day we encountered children still without proper medical care, families sleeping in the open, elderly people struggling to access food distribution points. Our physical exhaustion, combined with these overwhelming needs, led us to bicker about what our priorities should be. We all agreed people were suffering far too severely, still without access to essentials like clean water and food, and that months after the quake the coordination efforts were still taking too long. But each of us had our own fierce convictions about how to tackle these problems "better," and our passion often turned our strategy sessions into arguments.

Kim wanted to plant gardens in orphanages so kids would have something productive to do and also grow their own food. Malia had heard about an emerging technology to recycle rubble into concrete, and she wanted us to make bricks and focus on rebuilding homes. I too was drowning in the immediate needs of the Haitian people, but I was convinced we needed to look at the root causes of poverty. In those days we couldn't seem to agree on anything and it was easy to be unsettled by the chaos. Every issue we considered felt both urgent and overwhelming. Maybe the lifetime commitment that was necessary for any progress to be made was sinking in. We were falling apart and I was petrified. Had I made a terrible mistake, convincing my friends to abandon their comfortable lives and follow me into this? We were unraveling, and the weight of that responsibility kept me up at night. Our decision to be independent of any established organization allowed us certain freedoms—we could move quickly and without bureaucracy, getting quick returns on our work—but our small victories came with so many sacrifices. Each grueling day left us more exhausted than the last, and I couldn't shake the gnawing fear that we'd taken on more than we could handle.

Our first few weeks back in Haiti challenged us more than we anticipated, but Kim, Malia, and I kept pushing forward and never stopped working. Gradually we noticed the whispers rippling through the small disaster response community. In a world where most volunteers lasted only weeks before the harsh conditions drove them home, our continued presence was becoming impossible to ignore. We certainly weren't cut from the same cloth as the typical aid workers. We were an anomaly, particularly among the UN women, who somehow were always nicely dressed and looked fresh and clean, navigating rubble in heels and full makeup, while we embraced the grime of the work. Our sandals were caked with mud, our irregular bathing schedule left us far from fragrant, and our clothes bore the dust and sweat of each day's labor. Who were we working for? What was our mission? The questions circulated, but we didn't care; we just kept our heads down and our activities focused. Our determination paid off and our reputation grew as the weeks passed. We were the hardworking misfits who got things done—and in the end we had gained something invaluable, the respect of our comrades on the ground.

Although we continued to have frequent internal arguments, what we always agreed on was that our response needed to be flexible as circumstances changed around us every day. We wanted to learn how to do things better.

For me, this meant understanding what people in Haiti really needed from us. The survivors of this tragedy were already painfully aware of how this story would play out, just as it had every time there was a natural disaster in their country. Foreign workers would fly in and follow protocol by giving away rice, water, and tents, not understanding the long-term effects of giving without having a sustainability plan.

At first, every bag of rice I handed out felt like a small victory—another family fed, another immediate need met. But living in Haiti stripped away these simple certainties. The acts of pure charity revealed themselves as something more complex, more damaging. Each bag of rice I distributed wasn't just food for a hungry family; it was income stolen from a local farmer. I could imagine his compromised livelihood, walking home from work empty-handed, his crops unsold because no one would buy local rice when foreign aid was free.

The longer I stayed, the clearer the pattern of our unintended outcomes became. Well-meaning group after group would give away rice, build a church or an orphanage that couldn't be sustained, snap photos for their supporters back home, and then depart as quickly as they came, leaving a wake of unintended consequences. I was beginning to gain a deeper understanding of the realities facing the people of Haiti. This awakening didn't blind me to the crucial role of emergency response; when disaster strikes, people need immediate help to survive. It's just that simultaneously I was starting to think about what Haiti would look like after everyone had inevitably left.

The new friends we were making were so much more than earthquake survivors. They were artists, teachers, and entrepreneurs, and each one continued to patiently impart their deep wisdom and insight, teaching me to think about long-term development and building infrastructure. As they had experienced many times in the past after a disaster response ended, the poverty in Haiti would overwhelm their communities, and once again people would be without access to any basic necessities. As straightforward as these concepts were, I was unsure where I fit into this complicated picture. My eyes were opening to what Haiti would look like in a year, or five years, or ten years, if we didn't start focusing on the root problems of poverty, and I had a deep desire to reform the way I participated in the work here. I didn't know then what it would take to change the status quo of charitable aid and what would come of it all. I had no idea then how many meetings, interactions, and years it would take to build and implement the system we did finally create to start making those changes. I didn't even know where to begin.

Then one day, everything I had done and all my experiences in life began to make sense. During another relentless morning, Kim, Malia, and I were distributing water filtration systems in a local camp. Walking through the maze of tents, I felt a hand grab my arm. An older woman with a kind smile looked right into my eyes and said, "*Blan, mwen pa bezwen dlo, mwen vle travay.*" And then she smiled even more broadly and stroked my hair. I had no idea what she had said, but the affectionate and determined way she spoke haunted me. I wrote her words in my journal and thought about her all day. I couldn't get her face out of my mind.

Later, James translated her words as, "White lady, I don't want any water, but I need a job." I made him repeat it, over and over. Those words pierced the core of my being. A woman I never saw again taught me in that moment the most valuable lesson of all time. With the access I had as a foreign person and all the resources I could call upon, handing out water was not the solution to the poverty that was all around us. It was so simple and so obvious, and I became obsessed with the idea: stop giving things away, start creating jobs. Every day, as more rubble was cleaned from the streets, more enlightenment was being given to me. I was beginning to understand that disaster response and long-term development could coexist if we considered the root problems Haitian citizens were facing and we listened to their solutions.

I was changing in other ways, too. My tolerance for warm rum was increasing to impressive levels. In the end it seemed safer than drinking water, the quality of which was often questionable. I started smoking cigarettes to curb hunger and keep myself from dipping into the limited supply of tuna packets we had. Conditions at the airport base were deteriorating rapidly. Water supplies were dangerously low, everyone was getting sick, and we were reduced to taking "bucket showers," carrying our rationed quarter-bucket of water into the field to bathe.

Through conversations with other relief workers, Kim, Malia, and I learned that the United Nations Log Base had an endless supply of clean water. We had been there for meetings, and it was a stark contrast to our conditions at the airport. Since Log Base was the focal point of the rebuilding efforts and the most developed place in the neighborhood of Tabarre, we wondered how we could become permanent residents there. It felt audacious, maybe even impossible,

March 2010, Port-au-Prince, Haiti. Aline (woman to the left) and her family lived in this tent camp for over a year. After our charity, REBUILD globally, was officially established, her sons (two boys in photo) became students in our education program. Her friend, Enose, (woman to the right) has worked at our company, Deux Mains, for more than a decade.

but in those tough times, doing what was necessary became second nature.

Kim, Malia, and I meticulously prepared for our mission. We spent days conducting reconnaissance, studying the process of entering Log Base to discover how we could make a plan work. The base, serving countless purposes, was still so disorganized that security protocols were practically nonexistent. We noticed that other relief workers used simple plastic badges on lanyards to get past security. These badges weren't scanned or checked through a computer system; they were just flashed at the guards at the entrance. From what we could tell, having a badge, any badge, seemed to grant authority not just to enter Log Base but to live there as well. Clearly, we needed badges of our own. With no time to waste, I boarded a flight to West Palm Beach, Florida, and turned to the one person I could always count on, my mom. I knew the warrior spirit beneath her calm exterior would be up for the task.

One of the strongest women in my life, my mom gave me roots in equality, perseverance, and even my unconventional lifestyle. I was lucky to know early on that there was so much more to her than her work as a florist, a wedding cake designer at the bakery she owned with my dad, and an elementary schoolteacher. On rare, cherished occasions I'd catch glimpses of her adventurous past. A second glass of Malbec would loosen her tongue, and suddenly stories would spill out—tales of her youthful days hitchhiking across Europe, a life far removed from the careful routines of the present. What truly set her apart, though, was the way she managed to excel at everything she did without ever letting her work take her away from being a mom. She gave her all to my sisters and me, not just her time but her attention, her wisdom, and her unshakable belief in our potential.

Her gift for perfectionism didn't exactly make it into my DNA, however. I was the fast-paced type, the kind of person who believed in getting things done quick and dirty, trusting momentum to carry me through. I knew I'd blow it if I tried to handle this critical part of our Log Base scam myself. I'd rush it, cut corners, and probably leave a trail. My mom was the only person who could pull it off. Her attention to detail could orchestrate miracles.

My mom hadn't wanted me to go to Haiti in the first place. The images on TV were terrifying, and she couldn't imagine me being there. Nor was she thrilled to hear I had quit my job and sold my house at the age of thirty, but she was ready and waiting to use her Photoshop skills to help. Over the weekend, she got to work manufacturing phony ID badges. She designed them carefully, complete with headshots I had saved on our old Nokia phone, fictitious barcodes, and a made-up organization name: Haiti Disaster Volunteers. It wasn't the most creative title, but it sounded official enough to do the job.

Armed with our freshly minted credentials and our tent, we strode onto Log Base like we owned the place, doing our best to exude the confidence of people who belonged there. To our surprise, it worked. No one stopped us, no one questioned us, and we slipped right in. The base was bursting at the seams, with nearly all the UN workers who had survived the earthquake plus their team of new arrivals making it their home. Offices doubled as temporary hostels, with mattresses and cots packed against the walls. For those unable to claim a cot, tents sprawled across any available space in the grass and on the sidewalks, leaving little room for newcomers like us to set up camp.

After an hour of scouring every inch of the base, we finally located an unclaimed plot of land on the far southwest corner. An overpowering stench rose from a nearby canal filled with rancid water, trash, and plastic bottles, making it clear why others had avoided it. But we didn't care. It was a space to call our own, and for us it would become home. The putrid smell coming from the trash river did, however, inspire our first improvement project: a bridge. We scavenged a few old two-by-four planks from the back of the base and tied them together to create a makeshift overpass. Each night, our final steps home became a precarious balancing act as we crossed it, but it was a small price to pay for the convenience it provided. With our tent pitched and our tiny corner of Log Base claimed, we lived here officially, among the UN staff and members of other big organizations.

It wasn't lost on us that the earthquake had left no community in Haiti untouched. That included our newest neighbors, the United Nations staff members. Just over one hundred of their small team had died that day, and the loss was deeply felt. Living side by side with them, Kim, Malia, and I mourned their loss, but we were also being exposed to a side of their operation we had never seen before. It was hard to comprehend the vastness of their resources. Fleets of vehicles lined up at the base and rows of computers sat under a large tarpaulin workstation. Even so, politics appeared to be impeding their ability to act quickly.

While I understood the need for accountability, behind-the-scenes revelations made it painfully apparent that working toward the same goal didn't mean we all agreed on how to get there. Every meeting led by the UN staff felt like a battlefield. The layers of protocol, the endless forms, and the fixed deals with "preferred contractors" made my blood boil. I'd bite my tongue as long as I could until finally I'd erupt.

"You're telling me we need *three weeks* of approvals before we can fix a water pump?" My voice would echo in the room, met by feigned patience or blank stares. The arguments that followed were intense, leaving me drained and fuming every time.

It was clear we didn't belong. We stood out like sore thumbs, and not just in meetings. Even our walking around base seemed to ruffle feathers and draw disapproving looks. The polished relief workers with their branded vests and organizational clout didn't know what to make of us. We were the outsiders, the nobodies, intruding on their well-oiled operations. A few of the chatty UN women referred to us as "misfits," their words floating carelessly through the air before they turned back to their tight-knit cliques, shutting us out completely. The isolation was hard. We struggled to find our footing, and as the days dragged on, the weight of it all began to wear us down. There was no escaping the pressure. It stripped us bare, forcing us to face fears and flaws we'd long buried. My confidence wavered, unraveling thread by thread, and paranoia crept in like a shadow. The disapproving whispers gnawed at me, threatening to tip me over the edge.

The challenge wasn't just loneliness or frustration; it was also our desperation. Every dollar mattered, and we didn't have one to spare. Every delay felt like a betrayal of the people waiting for help. And yet the very systems designed to ensure fairness and efficiency were grinding everything to a halt. While the big agencies shuffled their papers, we were scrambling to get clean water to families that hadn't had a proper drink in days. It was maddening. Skirting the red tape felt like rebellion, like stealing back time the bureaucracy had robbed us of. The experience was a sobering reminder of how broken the system was, how the rules designed to help people were the same ones keeping them trapped.

I had to find ways to hold it together if I was going to make it through this experience. So, I started with the small things, finding slivers of solace in my strange, crumbling surroundings. Back home, I'd always been terrified of spiders. Here in Haiti, with buildings reduced to rubble, the creatures seemed to have claimed the earth for themselves. Insects scurried everywhere, spiders spun webs like curtains, and saucer-sized tarantulas roamed freely. They'd sneak up on us when we least expected it, their sudden appearances prompting screams and leaps that could have rivaled those of Olympians. At first I hated them, but then I decided to try something different: I named them. Each tarantula that crossed my path became a "Fred" or a "Betty." I told myself I loved them, that they were my tiny, misunderstood friends. It didn't entirely work; my heart still raced every time one scuttled too close. But the effort mattered. It was a reminder that even in the darkest, most unsettling moments, I could choose the way I faced the world. And maybe, just maybe, I could learn to embrace the misfit in me.

Naming tarantulas was only the first of the peculiar survival games I invented to adapt to our new reality. The bathroom situation, for instance, was quite literally a daily exercise in humility. Since we still had no actual facilities, squatting behind our tent was the norm. At first it was mortifying, but then I decided to turn the indignity into a fitness challenge. I imagined myself in a gym class, working on my glutes, and held each squat for an extra ten seconds. It was ridiculous but it made me laugh, and in a strange way it gave me a sense of control over the absurdity of it all.

Things were definitely better at Log Base, but the lack of comforts we once took for granted were still glaring. Comfortable bed? A dream. Refrigeration? Forget it. Our beverages were lukewarm at best, and more often than not I found myself sipping warm beer, telling myself it was the hydration my body needed. I'd even try to savor it, convincing myself that this was some sort of rustic luxury. But truth be told, the warm beer probably contributed to my frequent stomach troubles. Still, with few supplies and even fewer friends, we had no choice but to suck it up and keep going. Every sip, every squat, every "Betty" or "Fred" became part of the strange rhythm of survival. Life here forced me to let go of dignity and embrace humor where I could find it, because sometimes laughing at the absurd was the only thing that kept me sane.

No matter how hard I tried to adapt, there were a few things I simply couldn't get used to. The worst, by far, was the constant discomfort of going unwashed. I had never imagined that being dirty could hurt so much. My skin burned and cracked, the filth and relentless heat rashes spreading like an unwelcome second layer. The dust and grime embedded in every pore were inescapable, a daily reminder of the harshness of this place. The physical pain was one thing, but the thought of all the people who lived without access to showers every day cut even deeper. Then there was the tent; a flimsy barrier of plastic between me and the vast unpredictability of the world outside. I used to love camping, with the thrill of a weekend under the stars with family or friends in some safe, curated slice of nature. Back then, it felt like an adventure, a test of courage. Now courage seemed like a far-off dream. The tent offered no comfort, no safety, just a hollow sense of vulnerability.

As the days passed, my fear deepened. I knew the statistics of violence against women, and the base housed about thirty male relief workers for every female. That imbalance gnawed at me. Whether my fears were justified or not, I made it a point never to be alone. Truthfully, however, no one wanted to be alone in those times. Even if you managed to carve out a moment for yourself, it wasn't peaceful. The silence wasn't comforting; it was oppressive. Alone with your thoughts, you couldn't help but confront the discord within and around you. And that, perhaps, was the scariest thing of all.

For some, creativity is born of fear, boredom, or some other emotion, and thus the abandoned body of a 747 airplane soon turned into a bar at log base, serving local beer and Haitian rum. It was always packed in the evenings, since just about everyone wanted to escape whatever they had seen or heard in the day. I knew it was an unhealthy way to deal with emotions, but drinking away reality seemed to help. My tentmates visited this unconventional hot spot quite frequently. Most nights my body ached from physical exhaustion and I just wanted to go to bed, but my desire not to be alone drew me to join the others. Some nights I would plop down on the stairs, lay my head against the body of the plane, and fall asleep while waiting for last call. I was getting to know the other relief workers by this point and my fear of being alone was probably exaggerated, but I was still uncomfortable living in a tent. In my home in Orlando, I had had a locked door, deadbolt, and chain to secure me as I slept. My home in Haiti had only a zipper to protect me.

Humor did really turn out to be a saving grace. When the others in my group found out that I slept with my kitchen knives under my sleeping bag and Exacto knives in my bra and panties, my fear of being alone turned into comic relief. They teased me endlessly, thinking it was so strange that I was brave enough to come to Haiti alone but afraid to sleep in a tent, and I never lived it down. I felt happy to serve as the butt of everyone's jokes, though, because it took the focus off my underlying fears. After being teased I sometimes realized it was the first time I had smiled in hours or even days.

Everyone was doing what they needed to do to survive and accomplish their mission. Kim, Malia, and I were also able to start having productive conversations about the organization we wanted to create. They knew how much a long-term solution meant to me, and in the end I got my friends to agree that the poverty that existed in Haiti before the earthquake would continue to plague the country afterward if we didn't try to do something about it. Finally,

I wore down Kim and Malia and they were ready to throw their energy into the impossible dream of fighting for the economic freedom of the Haitian people. A shared focus on fighting the systems all around us began to take shape. We also started to be more kind and patient with ourselves, allowing space for trial and error. Building something new, something meaningful, wasn't a task to accomplish overnight. It would take time, but we knew that if we stayed fervent and true to the vision we shared, we would be okay.

As we ventured deeper into the camps and neighborhoods, still delivering supplies we'd scavenged, one refrain grew louder, impossible to ignore. It was as if the woman I'd met months earlier had gone on a campaign to share her message. "We just want to work" echoed from one corner to the next, voices layered with longing and pride. The children's faces told a quieter story, boredom etched into their features, their eyes scanning the streets for something—anything—to fill the void.

"Help us go to school," they begged, their voices small but insistent, like fragile flames refusing to be snuffed out. *School and jobs. School and jobs.* It became a repeating chorus, the unbroken rhythm of every camp, every neighborhood, every conversation. It was also our compass,pointing us toward what mattered most.

While walking around the city, we also encountered dozens of street kids, boys living and working on the streets because they were parentless or had been displaced by poverty and needed to earn money to help their family survive. Nearly all the big agencies had vehicles and none of their staff ever walked anywhere. This wasn't the same experience we were having. Without constant access to our friend's car, we walked a lot. As some of the only foreign women walking in the neighborhood, we were an anomaly to the kids. They watched us walking along the streets as intently as we watched them hustling the cars at the busiest intersections. They greeted us with quick smiles and outstretched hands. Never idle, they were washing the windows of the cars that passed, hoping for a *gourde* or two (the official currency) to be tossed out the window.

Gidson, a boy smaller than the rest, was eager to talk, in hopes we might have something to share. He would grab my hand as we walked down the street and smile, teaching us swear words in Creole. In time, he and his big brother Ashly started teaching us other words too so we could better communicate. When I grew curious about where all the girls were, Gidson told me boys worked the streets during the days and girls worked them at night. A new horror came to light that day, only reinforcing that poverty is always cruelest to the most vulnerable.

We had nothing material to offer the street children and our work didn't necessarily include their plight, but I became deeply connected with the boys on the airport road. I somehow managed to earn their trust, and we always found ways to get a laugh as we suffered together under the burning Haitian sun. Early one morning before the sun even rose, I heard familiar voices screaming my name and rocks were being thrown at the cement gate that surrounded Log Base. It was Ashly and a few of the other boys, crying and frantically trying to get my attention. Caught off guard, I ran outside so quickly I didn't realize I was barefoot. Ashly's brother, little

June 2010, Port-au-Prince, Haiti. A few of the boys who were living and working on the streets of Port-au-Prince. Some days we practiced reading and writing, while others we just hung out, spending time together.

Gidson, had been hit by a car and left for dead on the side of the road.

By the time I arrived he was barely breathing and covered in blood from head to toe. I scooped him up and moved closer to the road, frantically waving my arm to get the attention of the cars passing by. One after another, the UN vehicles drove by me. My throat was raw from screaming when a man in a beige pickup truck finally stopped. I could tell he was in a hurry, but I begged him to take us to the hospital. He helped me load Gidson into the passenger seat of his truck and sped away to Bernard Mev's private nonprofit hospital a few miles away from us. As I ran barefoot into the hospital with Gidson, I was greeted by a nurse who quickly took him in her arms and laid him on a wooden bed in the corridor of the overcrowded space. It was only the first of many serious accidents in which I would tend to these boys, but luckily this time Gidson recovered with only more scars to add to his collection.

CHAPTER 4

REBUILD GLOBALLY

If you have come to help me, you are wasting your time. But if you have come because your liberation is bound up with mine, then let us work together.
Aboriginal Activists Group

○

We met a lot of other people with distinct personalities living at Log Base, and as the weeks turned into months, we started to make stronger connections with them. Josh, a young relief worker from the Isle of Man, was among them, and he became a fast friend. With a strong British accent, a heart of gold, and a knack for finding things of sentimental value, Josh had come here like me, without any sort of formal support. He bounced around Port-au-Prince for weeks, lending a hand with his superb talent for carpentry where he could, until he too realized Log Base was the place where all efforts were coordinated. With his bold personality and networking skills, he was able to sneak on base as well. Although he was tentless and didn't have anywhere permanent to sleep at night, he still worked every day with anyone who needed a volunteer.

One of Josh's first jobs was assisting in a food drop being distributed by the World Food Program. He arrived at the site with the other volunteers and was horror-struck to find thousands of people who hadn't eaten in days. Within minutes the crowd realized the food was going to run out, and wildly hungry people charged the trucks, grasping at the bags of rice. The panic caused the police to start hitting people and pushing them back from the trucks. Many were hurt and never fed. The experience haunted Josh. After that day soldiers accompanied food drops, but even so, Josh knew this wasn't the right work for him.

Back at Log Base, he continued to attend meetings, shaking hands and exchanging stories with every new face he met. One day he crossed paths with a group of British responders working with a nonprofit called SASH. They'd just secured a grant from the UN and were gearing up for a massive building project. In those days, most projects revolved around erecting t-shelters (transitional shelters designed to move displaced families out of tents and into wooded structures that could provide a greater degree of protection from the weather.) With its new funding, SASH was about to oversee a base with twelve camps just outside the city and they needed support. When the team explained their vision, Josh eagerly signed on to help. For weeks he and the SASH team assembled shelters under the sun's burning gaze. When the final t-shelter had been secured, Josh returned to Port-au-Prince, ready to dive headfirst into his next mission.

It was during one of those long days at Log Base that we bumped into him. From the moment we met Josh, it was clear to Kim, Malia, and me that he was one of us, a rogue spirit navigating the chaos of post-quake Haiti without the constraints of a formal relief organization. Josh seemed tailor-made for every challenge we threw at him, and his frustration with the endless bureaucracy and glacial pace of the emergency response mirrored our own. There was no hesitation, no awkward small talk. We all clicked, our shared determination creating an instant bond. After hearing Josh didn't have a tent to sleep in, we had made a unanimous decision: he would move into ours. Just like that, our scrappy little team grew stronger, bolstered by someone who shared our relentless drive to make a difference, no matter how unconventional the path.

Along with his bag and some packs of local cigarettes, Josh brought a huge tortoise shell he had found on the beach in Leogane. He spoke about it like it was a prized relic, his face lighting up as he told stories of the days he had spent in that coastal town, about thirty kilometers west of Port-au-Prince. Josh had nothing but fond memories of the kindness he had experienced and the people he had met there, and somehow that shell became his tangible connection to it all. I didn't want to take that away from him, but the problem with tortoise shells is, they rot.

Our tent was not made for extreme heat to begin with, so no matter what we did it was sweltering, and the smell was barely tolerable with just us dirty women in residence. Sweat and damp clothes had become part of our existence, but when the shell entered the picture, along with Josh, the stench reached an entirely new level. Words can't quite capture the suffocating aroma that seeped from our little plastic shelter. Although Josh could admit the smell was becoming toxic, it was hard for him to give up his shell. We sympathized but made it clear: it was us or the shell. Josh made the right choice and parted with his memento.

Another of our new allies, Jean Marc, was a force of nature in a different way than Josh. He was like a combination of celebrity chef Gordon Ramsay on one of his fiery tirades, mixed with a touch of inappropriate commentary often heard from US TV host Bill O'Reilly. Jean Marc wasn't the kind of man you forgot. His voice alone could cut through the loudest room, and his presence was impossible to ignore. A merchant to his core, Jean Marc had dabbled in nearly every industry Haiti had to offer over the past twenty years. From import-export deals to bustling markets, his ventures were as diverse as his personality. Most recently, he had thrown himself into the restaurant business, dominating the culinary scene in Haiti with an empire of eateries.

The crown jewel of Jean Marc's enterprises was a small, unassuming outdoor café perched at Log Base, aptly named The Deck. The Deck had somehow survived the earthquake and was one of the first restaurants to reopen after the disaster. It wasn't much, just a scattering of tables and chairs under the open sky, but it was the most normal and familiar place I had visited in Haiti, and one of the few spots on the base where weary workers could escape the chaos for a strong cup of coffee or a warm meal. To accommodate the constant smoking of all the response workers, each table held multiple ashtrays sitting next to the salt and pepper shakers. Jean Marc ran The Deck like a general commanding an army. He barked orders at his staff with military precision while charming his customers with his charisma and bold humor.

Jean Marc was the kind of man you wanted in your corner. He was so influential and well connected that only a few weeks after the disaster he was able to import fresh food and provide an actual menu of options. It was very fancy compared to the UN cafeteria, the economical choice where we had been grudgingly eating most of our meals. Even though we didn't have the money to eat at The Deck, we were desperate for the comfort of its mist-blowing fans and internet access, so we made excuses to hang out at a table in the far back of the café. We kept our heads down and thought we were hidden, but we were wrong. Jean Marc was acutely aware we were using his tables and chairs as our office.

One particularly hot afternoon he stomped toward our table and snarled in his strong French accent, with cigarette smoke coming from his nose. "Who are you people? Why do you think you can sit at my restaurant every day and only order coffee? I am not a charity."

We smiled and tried to use our charm to give ourselves a few more minutes in our unconventional office. Not impressed with our appeals, he insisted we leave immediately. We packed up our computers and water bottles and made our way out. Coming back the following day, we tried to blend in more and stay out of his way, but the lists of complaints Jean Marc had with us grew. He went on and on about how we couldn't just sit there all day taking up valuable dining space.

This pattern went on for weeks. We always knew when he had had enough of us, because the floor would start to shake when he was charging toward our table to tell us to order food or get out. Then something started to change, and to this day we don't know why, but Jean Marc began to be less angry about our presence and more admiring of our persistence. He yelled at us only occasionally now, and sometimes he brought us leftover fries or fruit from the lunchtime rush. Somehow, we were wearing him down. We finally made a deal with him: if we left during mealtimes, he would allow us to stay at our little table when the restaurant wasn't busy, and he wouldn't yell at us. He even promised not to complain about our existence to the other patrons in the restaurant.

As our relationship grew, we would catch Jean Marc's ear every once in a while, and tell him stories about our experiences living on base. One afternoon the three of us were loudly discussing what had just happened at the UN cafeteria when Jean Marc stomped over to our table.

"What is so funny?" he demanded.

Kim was laughing so hard she could barely get the words out of her mouth. Between gasps of breaths she sputtered, "Jules ate oatmeal from the cafeteria that was covered in bugs."

Jean Marc couldn't believe what she was saying. With his love of food and excellent service, he couldn't contain himself. He stood up angrily and threw an ashtray toward the UN cafeteria, yelling at the building walls as if they were transparent and he could see the cooks inside.

"You aren't chefs, you are all animals!" he screamed. Taken aback, I thanked him for being as disgusted as I was, while everyone else just laughed.

The next day and for the entire rest of the month, Jean Marc fed Malia, Kim, Josh, and me breakfast, lunch, and dinner. I don't know where this spirit of generosity came from, but it was the most incredible gift. Angry Jean Marc had become the head chef and main source of support for our group of misfits.

For months we'd managed to live illegally in our makeshift campsite, flying under the radar, and now enjoying the most familiar food Port-au-Prince had to offer us, but our time was soon up and our eviction was set in motion by none other than Tony, a UN staffer who had become another one of our few allies on the base. Tony had been with the United Nations in Haiti for many years and was intrigued by us outcasts. Several times a week he would invite us into his shipping-container office. He wanted to learn more about what we were doing in Haiti, and as we shared our wild tales, he shared his stash of rum, kept safe in the second drawer of his metal filing cabinet.

Tony's home in Pétion-Ville, perched in one of the city's more beautiful neighborhoods, had somehow survived the earthquake's wrath. He and his housemates had too, but not unscathed. A few of them carried the weight of trauma, haunted by their escape from the collapse of the Hotel Montana, a favored meeting spot for the UN staff and a graveyard for so many of their colleagues. As the days stretched into weeks, the housemates couldn't take it anymore. The memories of the Montana and the crumbling city around them became too much. One by one, they packed their bags and departed Haiti, leaving Tony to navigate the ruins of his world alone. Sometimes I think that's why he befriended us so quickly when others shunned us, but the reasons we became friends were immaterial. In those days, finding good friends meant everything. Some moments in Haiti were like hell on earth, and even though we all quickly got used to it, the love we had for each other got us through the toughest times. None of us took our bonds for granted.

One day Tony asked us how we had lived at Log Base so long without being caught, and I showed him our badges and bragged about my mom's forgery skills. We even proudly led him right to our little hidden camp and told stories about how we spent our nights there where the weather seemed to taunt us. We told him how the relentless rain turned the area into a muddy swamp most of the time. We wore our Wellington boots to keep the mud off our pants, but even so, it was impossible to keep our tent clean. Between the mud from torrential downpours, our sweat from hours of unforgiving heat, and Josh, there was a lot to be desired. In spite of the drawbacks, however, we were proud of our setup, glad that living at the base and attending the cluster meetings was giving us relevant information about the plans of the big organizations. We were learning a lot.

That afternoon, however, Tony's white work truck with its unmistakable blue UN badge arrived at our camp. It stopped right before our little two-by-four bridge, and Tony jumped out and ordered us to pack our bags and come with him. I didn't recognize his mood and couldn't tell whether we were in trouble because of our fake badge scheme.

In silence Tony drove us through the streets, still broken and rubble-filled, taking mostly back roads and shortcuts. I was seeing communities I hadn't seen before, even though we went only a short distance. I couldn't believe how many people lived in these little hideaway areas. Tents lined both sides of the roads, still damp from the last night's rain, and exhausted people were everywhere, trying to get dry.

The rubble may have shifted, but the suffering was constant. We ended up on one of the main roads, Route de Frères, and came upon the Djoumbala Night Club and Casino, which didn't look as though it had sustained much earthquake damage. Behind the club was a beautiful community of homes, most of them destroyed, but you could tell it had once been a prominent neighborhood.

A few of the homes made from rebar and concrete had stood strong, and luckily Tony rented one of them. He helped us take our few belongings from his truck and set them in a small bedroom inside. It seemed we were moving in. I was baffled, but Tony was adamant that we could no longer stay at Log Base. He said there was a reason no one lived on that little plot of land we had called home for so many days and nights, but he still wouldn't tell us what it was.

After we got settled in our new room, Tony sat us down at his dining room table and poured us each a shot of rum. His face was ghastly and his tone grim as he finally explained.

"An emergency tent-hospital was set up at Log Base right after the earthquake," he began. He paused and took a deep breath. "Medics were forced to perform hundreds of amputations, and without a plan for safe disposal, those body parts needed to be buried quickly to avoid any further disease."

"Wait," I interrupted, aghast. "The place where we set up our tent is the burial site of those body parts?"

"I'm sorry to say so." Tony chugged back his shot of rum. "The area was immediately quarantined."

We had had no idea what lay beneath us. The ground we stood on, the floor we slept on, were steeped in horrors we couldn't begin to imagine. Tony allowed us to stay without conditions while we searched for a new place, his house serving as a temporary escape from the madness that surrounded us. The news hit us all differently. Josh didn't last long in the house. His sensitive and adventurous spirit soon took him back to Leogane, while we took our time to find a new home base. We never spoke of this time again, but every day we were confronted by living reminders as people who were missing limbs and needed medical care walked the streets.

Six months into our work, our trio was about to become a duo when Malia decided it was time to return to the States to start a family. Kim and I supported her, but losing her was difficult. She was the toughest among us, the one who never broke under the weight of the work. Without her, I felt even more pushed beyond my limits, especially with the continued medical crises surrounding us. Reprieve came, however, when I started forming connections with nurses and doctors from smaller organizations. These groups operated with a quiet resilience, and working alongside them created a deep sense of camaraderie, plus I needed additional emotional support to keep going, especially with Malia gone.

When we met Nurse Beth, a seasoned trauma nurse, her friendship became pivotal. She ran the clinic at the Pétion-Ville Golf Course, a medical outpost set up by actor Sean Penn, and she was relentless. Every patient who crossed her path, every wound, every broken body—she met them all with focus and determination.

Beth wasn't alone in this grueling work. She was usually accompanied by her sidekick Maeve, a fiery Irish nurse whose sharp wit and steady hands made her the perfect counterpart to Beth's quiet intensity. Together, they worked as if the weight of the world rested on their shoulders, because in many ways it did. Even though I learned early on that I was not suited for any sort of medical work, I became a familiar face at their clinic, walking through their doors with women who had nowhere else to turn or injured children who clung to my hand.

One day I met a young woman who had endured the agony of untreated UTIs for far too long. When I got her to the clinic I could see the fear in her eyes, but Beth was a pro; she reassured her, spoke gently, explained the procedure of injecting her with a huge needle of antibiotics, and got to work. My role was simple enough: hold the woman's arm and offer whatever comfort I could. I did my best to steady her and pat her back, but when that needle pierced her skin, I suddenly felt the room spinning. Before I could stop myself, I crumpled to the ground, fainting right there in front of them.

Beth glanced at me briefly but she didn't stop what she was doing. Maeve threw me a look but didn't say a word. They were used to this sort of archaic medicine and I still wasn't, flinching at every improvised procedure. Even knowing my sensitive disposition, Beth never shielded me from the difficult cases. Nothing, however, prepared me for what was coming, a challenge that would force me to confront the very edges of what I thought I could handle.

I was working in a camp when Boot, a street kid I had gotten to know, came limping towards me, his face tight with pain. He was only eleven years old when the earthquake had taken his leg, and though he always carried himself with a quiet strength, today something was different and I immediately called Beth.

"Beth, it's Boot," I said, my voice barely steady. "Something's wrong with his leg."

"I'm in the middle of treating dozens of women, Julie. I can't make it down to Tabarre today," she told me calmly. "But I'll do an assessment over the phone. I need you to carefully unwrap the gauze that's covering Boot's stump."

I could smell his rotting flesh before I finished unwinding the layers of cloth. "Beth," I screamed into my old Nokia phone, "he needs help!"

"So help him, Julie" she replied, her voice composed but with intention. She then guided me through the process of cleaning and rebandaging Boot's leg. The next morning she and Maeve arrived at the compound with a garbage bag full of supplies. They told me the wound needed to be washed and rebandaged daily, and since Boot was a street kid without anyone else to do this for him, I would have to learn how to do it properly. The nurses taught me what I needed to know, and for a few weeks Boot came over every morning and I cleaned his stump. He worked hard to ensure he didn't get another infection, which was a real task considering the way he lived.

I was constantly reminded how challenging life was for these boys, and whatever I did was not enough to help change their situation in any real way. I never had the sort of facility or training to provide what these kids really needed: a way to get off the streets permanently. Over the years, we were able to help fit Boot with different prosthetic legs, but most of the ones donated were rejects from the United

States. They were uncomfortable old-fashioned limbs, and they always ended up making his condition worse.

I struggled, and still do, over my relationships with the street boys. Boot's prosthetics were a kind of metaphor for my participation in their lives. As so often in Haiti, what I thought I could do to make things better turned out not to be the solution needed to heal pervasive and complicated wounds. Boot learned to work the streets and live his life, with his old metal crutch serving as his right leg, and I continued to be his friend.

Haiti was teaching me lessons I never expected to learn, about why certain systems exist, how they persist, and the uphill battle required to change them. This earned knowledge gave me the perspective I needed to make thoughtful decisions about where I believed I could make an impact. But knowing didn't make it easier. Each discovery was heavy, each truth a new weight to carry. Nurse Beth continued to be a steady presence during those days. She always stepped in when I brought a patient to her clinic, which happened more often than I had anticipated. Beth always moved quickly, her no-nonsense demeanor a stark contrast to the turmoil surrounding us.

One day I walked into the clinic with yet another emergency, but this time something in *me* felt off. It wasn't just the difficult situation or the sight of injuries. It was something deeper, a sort of hopelessness. Beth looked up from her work and caught my eye. She didn't say anything right away, but her expression softened.

"You okay?" she asked, her voice cutting through the buzz of the clinic. I nodded automatically, but she didn't buy it.

"You look like you've been hit by a truck." I laughed weakly, but the sound didn't feel real. "Just tired," I said, though that wasn't the truth. Beth didn't press me, at least not then. But she kept an eye on me that day, her quiet way of showing that she understood

The following Sunday morning, Beth drove me up the Delmas 33 road to a small, two-story house with open windows and a tile floor. There were about 20 chairs in a semicircle and a guitar leaning up against the wall. This was a house church that some volunteers and locals had created as a safe place for people to worship. There was no sermon, just people talking, so it felt more like a small group meeting. At first, I was a little uncomfortable. My relationship with God was strained. Unexpectedly, I lost control when a young man picked up the guitar and started singing *God Is So Good*. Before I knew it, everyone was holding hands. I didn't feel judged for the endless tears that rolled down my face. I just felt supported and loved.

My words faltering as I wiped the tears away with my arm, I told the group about the street kids I had come to know. I spoke about the things they had confided to me, and how I was struck to realize they all wanted the same thing: beyond longing for safety and a family, they wanted to go to school. As I spoke, the weight of it all came crashing down. I was powerless, and saying it out loud felt like admitting defeat.

The room was quiet when I finished. No one rushed to offer solutions or platitudes. They just sat with me in the moment, unflinching, their presence a quiet balm. It was in that stillness, surrounded by people who, like me, had no answers, that I felt a flicker of courage I hadn't felt in a while. It wasn't grand or overwhelming, just a small flame, but something about the way they prayed, the way they clung to hope despite all the terrible things happening in Haiti, encouraged me to make a profound decision. Education, I knew, was a critical step in breaking the cycle of poverty. I spoke with Kim and we agreed our nonprofit would do many things to help people get back to school and work, and the time had come to take action. We would somehow help the kids we were interacting with return to school.

I knew building a shiny new school wasn't the answer; we needed to ground our efforts in partnerships with local people. The existing system wasn't perfect; in fact, it was deeply flawed, but it was already there, and it was what we had to work with. We didn't need to replace it; we needed to strengthen it. It was humbling to admit how small I felt and how little we had to work with, but our size didn't have to be a limitation. If we used the new knowledge we were acquiring, it could be our advantage. If we wanted our nonprofit to work differently than those we had watched fail, we needed to work in tandem with the schools that were reopening in the aftermath of the disaster. I had heard there were small groups throughout the camps running on sheer passion, teachers using tarps as chalkboards, administrators working to organize students every day, unpaid, simply because they cared about educating the children. Their grit was inspiring, but grit alone couldn't keep classrooms open.

That evening I sat cross-legged on the concrete floor outside Tony's house scribbling acronyms for the name of our nonprofit organization. With a cigarette in one hand and a Prestige in the other, I exhaled slowly, staring at the scrap of paper in my lap, covered in half-formed ideas. I was trying to capture something bigger than relief work, something that spoke to renewal, to dignity. I played around for a few hours, letting the letters dance in my mind until they finally clicked. REBUILD: Restoring Environments by Utilizing Innovative Local Development. My pulse quickened. That would be the name of our charity organization. I tacked on *globally* at the end, daring to dream that someday we would have an organization that might ripple across the world. There it was, REBUILD globally, a name and a credo for our charity.

I pressed the paper flat, running my fingers over the words. I had seen too many well-intentioned efforts pour into Haiti only to disappear when the next crisis stole the world's attention. REBUILD globally would be different. We would create something that empowered and honored the people of Haiti and supported the systems they had in place. As the night deepened, I kept scribbling the words *school* and *jobs,* sketching rough diagrams, swatting at mosquitoes that hovered in the humid air. My mind raced, thinking about the shift from disaster response to a plan that would support education and eventually job creation.... this was just the beginning.

Kim and I began designing our first program, which we called Elèv, to partner with the local schools that were working in the camps. Elèv means *student* in Creole. By covering the tuition for just a few students, we could help pay teachers' salaries, keeping the system afloat. We would also offer students a Saturday class to enforce classroom lessons and introduce extracurricular activities that focused on teamwork and community building. It was a small but powerful intervention, and one that was in tune with Haiti's culture. My time here had taught me how deeply rooted the spirit of sharing is. That norm gave me hope. With every tuition we covered, we weren't going to help just one student; we would help strengthen the system. This was how REBUILD globally began to take shape, not through grand gestures but through small, intentional actions rooted in the belief that the education of individual students could support entire classrooms.

CHAPTER 5

JOLINA

*If you give me food today, tomorrow my children will be hungry.
If you give me a job, my children will have food every day.*
   Jolina Desroches

○

After seven solid months in Haiti, I was beginning to adapt to the rhythm of my new existence. The memory of my life in the United States was fading, replaced by the constant, grinding pulse of survival. Kim and I cycled through a string of tent camps, and after the brief stint in Tony's house we landed back in a tent at a small compound called Grassroots United. It was a place designed to bring foreigners and Haitians together, a staging ground for projects before they reached the communities they were meant to serve. It was nostalgic for me in a way, reminding me of my old job in Orlando, where eager volunteers could find their footing before diving headfirst into the work. The compound filled a void for us by offering a safe place to live, work, and continue planning our nonprofit venture.

By day Kim and I distributed goods to families still struggling to survive, navigating the maze of need and urgency. By night we sat together, sketching out more plans for REBUILD globally's Elèv program. The work consumed us, but the compound gave us the tools to press forward and just enough stability to dream about what came next. I was getting comfortable with our new life, maybe too comfortable, as ludicrous accidents now felt like just another part of the day, expected, almost normal.

Kim and I didn't have much to call our own, but we shared everything we did have. Living with so little had a strange effect on us. It made us generous in a way we'd never been before, as though the lack of possessions loosened our grip on the idea of ownership itself. At the same time, it made us fiercely protective of a few things we became strangely attached to. For me, it was my notebook. I couldn't go anywhere without it. I felt exposed, almost naked, if it was not by my side. For Kim, it was hot sauce. She kept packets of it tucked away and brought them out at every meal, dousing whatever food we could find. Then there were the pajama pants. They weren't much to look at, just a soft pair of lightweight bottoms that had probably seen better days. But in a life where comfort was rare, those pants were a treasure. They kept us cool in the blistering heat, and we both claimed them whenever we needed a little relief.

One day I was wearing the pants when another nasty stomach bug hit me. It came on quickly, and by some miracle I made it to the compost toilet in time. As the hours wore on, however, my luck ran out and I had an accident in our beloved pants. Weak and mortified, I rinsed them in my bucket of water and hung them on a wooden post to dry. I told myself I'd go back later and wash them properly when I felt stronger. But later that evening, as I lay in a daze, I glanced over and froze. Kim was wearing the pants. I was horrified, but I couldn't bring myself to say anything. My voice caught in my throat and I turned away, hoping she wouldn't notice my flushed face. The next day I threw myself back into work as if nothing had happened. We had been through so much together, but this experience was over the top. I vowed never to tell her about the pants, believing that life in Haiti didn't leave much room for reflection or embarrassment. Hopefully the statute of limitations is up, because I guess she knows now.

Living at Grassroots United opened us up to a new network of friends, fellow responders who, like us, weren't planning to leave anytime soon but who also didn't work for the large organizations or the UN. Among them was Emma, a spirited British woman with an infectious laugh and a no-nonsense attitude. Emma and her fiancé Andy had founded an organization called International Disaster Volunteers (IDV). Their charity focused on finding practical solutions after disasters struck, and they were as committed as anyone I'd met. Their base was just down the road from ours, so we often crossed paths. Without a car, we were confined to our neighborhood, and essential friendships took shape quickly.

One particularly sweltering morning, I stood stirring donated baby formula into my coffee. It wasn't ideal, but it was the only creamer substitute we had. Emma appeared behind me, smirking. "When are you going to learn to drink coffee black and stop stealing from the babies?" she teased.

"When you stop judging my survival tactics," I laughed, waving her off. "How's your day going?"

She leaned against the counter, her tone more serious but still excited. "Pretty good, actually. I just met someone who reminds me of you. She's as obsessed with job creation as you are."

"Oh, yeah?" I asked, intrigued.

"She's amazing. Her name's Jolina, and you *have* to meet her," Emma said, her eyes lighting up. "Promise me you'll make it happen."

Just a few blocks from where I was living, Jolina was running an orphanage for children whose parents had died in the earthquake. I soon learned she was a hometown hero, a pillar of strength in her community of Tabarre even before the earthquake had brought such wreckage. The president of a local women's group, Jolina dedicated herself to teaching safe birthing techniques and family planning to women in the neighborhood and empowered them with life-saving knowledge. In town meetings her voice carried above the din as she stood toe-to-toe with her male counterparts, fearlessly championing the rights of women and the needs of the vulnerable. In times of hardship, it was Jolina who rallied her neighbors, ensuring no one was left behind.

Her modest home in Tabarre reflected the life she had made with her husband Smith and their two daughters, Mikaielle and Esther. Built with sturdy concrete blocks, it stood beneath a corrugated tin roof, its kitchen outside to keep the heat from seeping into the living space. For four years the house had been the family's safe haven, a simple but charming place where love outshone the cracks in the walls. But all that changed in an instant. Mikaielle was five and Esther three when their home was reduced to rubble in the quake.

The neighborhood they had always called home had been shaped by centuries of triumph and hardship. Tabarre was once a fertile floodplain where figs, bananas, and sweet potatoes thrived, sustaining generations of families who worked its soil. Its heart, however, lay in the sugarcane fields. For centuries sugarcane had tied Haiti to the brutal machinery of colonialism, its sweet harvest built on the backs of enslaved Africans who toiled in unimaginable suffering. Sugarcane was not just a commodity; it was a symbol of exploitation and defiance.

It was here, in these fields, that whispers of rebellion grew into shouts of revolution. Haiti's fight for independence, the first successful enslaved people's revolt in history, left its mark on every corner of the land, including Tabarre. But even as the nation broke free of its colonial masters, the scars remained, weaving a legacy of resilience and loss. Today the area's painful past is memorialized in Sugar Cane Historical Park, a centerpiece of Tabarre. The park stands as a dual symbol: of pride in Haiti's endurance and of the victims to whose lives it bears witness.

In the 1990s, however, Tabarre's fertile agricultural lands were sacrificed to the construction of Boulevard 15 Octobre, a highway that was supposed to be a symbol of progress, an artery to connect Tabarre to opportunities in the capital and beyond. But to Jolina, it felt more like a knife slicing through her home. Fields that had once been alive with farmers harvesting sugarcane and sweet potatoes were suddenly divided by miles of concrete.

The highway brought businesses, office buildings, and eventually the towering US Embassy. The fields withered, and the community that had once thrived on self-reliance had to find other ways to survive. Some neighbors turned to selling goods by the roadside, while others sought jobs in the new offices. Few were hired.

Jolina found her livelihood in the bustling street market of Tabarre, where life hummed with the chatter of negotiations and the aroma of street food. A natural salesperson with an easy wit, she sold soap, perfume, deodorant, and toothpaste from a small stall in Tét Béf, one of the rare covered markets whose name, meaning "cow's head" in Creole, added a rustic charm to its chaotic vibrancy. Every morning, Jolina rose early to balance the demands of running her business and raising two small children. Mikaielle was just starting school, and Esther still needed her mother's constant care. Jolina's niece often stopped by after school to help sell goods, while Soul, a close family friend, arrived early to open the stall, giving Jolina precious extra moments to ready Mikaielle for the school day.

The marketplace was a lifeline for Jolina's family, just a few miles away from the house they rented, and it provided the steady income that kept her family afloat. Jolina's husband Smith had his own source of pride, a tap-tap business. These colorful buses or pickup trucks, outfitted with vibrant designs and makeshift roofs to shield passengers from the Caribbean sun, are the lifeblood of Haiti's public transportation system. Smith had rented the same tap-tap for years and had covered the same route in Tabarre from Petite Place Cazeau to Trois Mains, just a stone's throw from the international airport.

It was a life built on hustle and hope, on squeezing joy from the mundane and the routine. But when the earth trembled violently for thirty-five seconds, everything changed. Jolina barely escaped the market with her life, her stall reduced to rubble in an instant. Smith's tap-tap fared no better. On the very route that had fed their family for years, an enormous block of concrete fell and crushed the truck beyond repair. In a single day, both parents had lost their livelihoods. The security they had painstakingly built was gone, leaving them to wonder how to feed their children and rebuild with nothing.

Not long after Emma told me about Jolina, I arranged to meet her at the orphanage she had cobbled together from tarpaulins. Making the journey there was like walking through the graveyard of a broken city. The dirt road was littered with wreckage, crushed and abandoned cars rusting into the earth and skeletal buildings with jagged rebar jutting out like exposed nerves. The orphanage, however, was a testament to resilience amid devastation. Its tattered tarp walls and ceiling were weathered by months of relentless Haitian storms and sagged under the weight of mold and wear. They were barely held together by fraying strings. The air smelled of dampness and decay, and the ground was slick with the mud of recent floods, mingling with streams of trash that coursed through the narrow alleyways.

Yet Jolina greeted me with a smile so warm, so full of strength, that it immediately disarmed me, brightening the makeshift space in which we stood. The sun beat down relentlessly, but there she was, speaking with a grace and dignity that seemed untouched by the world around her. She spoke of the Red Cross and the life-saving aid that had come to her camp. As she talked, she pointed to the edges of the room, where the walls were little more than the shredded remains of old tents. I inhaled sharply, my stomach tightening as I took in the sight. I had seen poverty, but this kind of raw, exposed space for so many children left me shocked. Yet it had given Jolina's family something they hadn't had since the earthquake: shelter.

Jolina paid no attention to my drifting eyes shocked by the black mold creeping along the sides of the tent, curling in the corners where the seams met the floor. "By the grace of God," she said, "a random distribution of rice, oil, or clothes may appear in my camp. And for this I feel so much gratitude But, Julie ... these distributions are fewer and farther apart. I cannot survive on charity alone." Her voice was steady but laced with concern. She went on to describe how she and her husband couldn't rebuild and were powerless without an income or opportunity to work. They were 100-percent dependent on the drifting charity that might or might not come their way.

"It's not enough," she said, shaking her head slowly. "We need a way to work, to rebuild, to create. We need opportunity. We need jobs." She looked at me, eyes wide with determination.

Jolina was speaking a truth I had been struggling to articulate since I met the woman in the camp who didn't want water but needed a job. She was setting the stage for the second initiative our charity could undertake. We could partner with Haitian women to fill the holes that made it difficult to get and maintain sustainable jobs. If we worked together to create something new, focused on financial freedom for those who had lost everything, people like Jolina could stand on their own two feet once again.

I paused, gathering my thoughts. And then impulsively I said, "I've been dreaming about something I experienced in South Africa that changed me. I saw artisans turning old tires into sandals. They'd take the walls of discarded tires they found on the streets and shape them into soles. Covering the top with local fabric, they sold them in the marketplace. It seems like they were simple enough to make. These craftspeople, they didn't need much..."

Jolina's face was transformed. Her eyes lit up with recognition, and before I could finish, she took both my hands in hers, holding them firmly as if our words had already created a bond that needed no translation. "There are many tires in Haiti," she said, her voice soft but filled with conviction. "They are burned here, thrown away as trash." I nodded, my heart racing. "We could learn how to do this ourselves," I said, my voice gaining strength. The idea was taking root in my mind, and I couldn't stop it now. Jolina squeezed my hands tighter, pulling me closer, her gaze unwavering. "I once worked in a factory," she said. "And I can sew."

I took a deep breath. "Jolina," I said, "I'm not from a big organization. I don't have a lot of resources or a well-funded program. I have already promised to help kids get back to school, but I want to create jobs with you as well. I just don't have a lot of money." My words etched in fear didn't seem to affect her at all. "We will take back everything the earthquake stole from us," she whispered, as if the very words had power. "We will teach people to make sandals from these tires, give them skills, and show them a craft they can call

July 2010, Port-au-Prince, Haiti. From the onset of our friendship, Jolina brought me to community meetings, introducing me to local Haitian groups working on issues such as women's health, child welfare, and economic development, always shining as a great leader.

their own. We will make our own money. This is how we begin to rebuild."

As Jolina and I continued to fantasize together, my attention drifted again to the children. Some were playing in the dirt outside. Inside the tent were four army cots, each holding several young children while the older ones sat on the floor. Their tiny hands passed around a single bowl, taking turns with one spoon as they shared the little rice they had. A small boy, no older than two, took a tiny bite and then spoon-fed the little girl to the left of him. She was even younger than he, her face still round and innocent. The boy then passed the bowl and spoon to the next little girl, who waited patiently for her turn. I had never seen anything like this before. The instinctive good nature of these children who had lost everything, even their parents, humbled me.

Jolina ignored my distracted state. "We need to focus on the women," she said. "They're the backbone of the family here in Haiti. They're the ones who keep things together." Her words snapped me back into the present and I met her gaze. She was right. As much as I had seen the struggles of the children, it was the women who could hold the key to real, lasting change. They were the ones who would rebuild their homes, their communities, and ultimately their country.

Jolina's proposal was simple: she would work with the local pastor and her women's group to put together a team of women who could learn the craft of sandal making. I would bring the materials, and most importantly the training manual. My brief encounter with artisans in South Africa making sandals from tires was nothing more than a starting point, however. I needed to gather more knowledge, find the right resources, and build a system that could make this work. But my skills were not in craftsmanship—they were in nonprofit management. Before we moved forward with our plans, we'd need to raise funds for the two programs we saw coming to life: scholarships for young people to go back to school and sandal-making training for women.

After some time to think it over, I decided the best plan forward would be to host our first official charity event to fund our new initiatives. With a strong network in Orlando, I knew I had the support I needed, and I leaned heavily on friends and connections to pull it all together. A local arts center near my old home in Orlando generously donated its space to us. The plan for our first fundraiser was bold: to temporarily transform the beautiful arts center into a post-earthquake neighborhood. We recreated the destruction with fake rubble made from papier-mâché and set up tents throughout the space, mimicking the conditions in Haiti. I wanted people to walk in and instantly feel the gravity of what had happened, to understand the stark reality in which we were working.

A month later the planning was finished, and we invited important guests, particularly from the Haitian community in Orlando, hoping to build new support and connections. I was excited. This was my chance to share our mission, to tell the world what REBUILD globally was doing differently in Haiti. I wanted people to know that we weren't going to throw money at a broken system and hope for the best. We were there to create something lasting, opportunities to develop skills so women could join a workforce and take back their futures, and to support the local school system so children could get back to school.

As I took the mic in front of the large crowd that day, a wave of nerves hit. But I cleared my throat and began. "We're here tonight to tell you about our plans to rebuild, not just with temporary relief, but with sustainable, long-term solutions." I paused, gathering my thoughts. "We've partnered with Haitian schools to provide scholarships for kids to attend, helping schools reopen and ensuring teachers get paid. It's meant to have a double impact, supporting education and helping communities thrive." I could feel the energy in the room shift as people began to understand the depth of our mission. Now for the second part.

"We're also training local Haitian women to make sandals from recycled tires. It's a simple yet powerful way to invest in skills and create jobs in communities where they're desperately needed. This isn't just about charity. It's about putting money back in the hands of Haitian people and giving them the tools they need to succeed."

As I spoke, I saw the heads nodding in agreement. This was the real impact we had been striving for, a vision that wasn't just about aid but also fostered empowerment and opportunity. I wrapped up my remarks, feeling a deep sense of gratitude.

"Thank you all for being here tonight. This event is incredibly special to me, as it brings together my two worlds, our amazing nonprofit community here in Orlando, and the new chapter I've started in Haiti. Your support tonight and in the years to come will help us not only establish our foundation but ensure that our impact lasts." The applause that followed felt like more than just appreciation; it felt like a promise. We were on the right path, and with the generosity and continued support of our community, REBUILD globally would grow and make a lasting difference in Haiti.

Without a passport Jolina couldn't join Kim and me in Orlando for the fundraiser, so she remained in Haiti, keeping the vision alive on the ground. Despite the distance, we kept in constant communication, and I could feel the energy and determination in her every message. During one of our conversations, Jolina noted how much work each of the programs would take to get off the ground and decided we needed to divide our efforts. "Kim's heart is with the kids," she said. "I think she should lead the program to get them back in school." Her insight was clear. Kim had formed a strong bond with the children, and this could be her focus.

Jolina also believed she and I were better suited to zero in on the job-training aspect and I agreed. Over the next few weeks, our conversations grew more focused and strategic, and our plan for the sandal-making program started to take clearer shape. We were going to host training classes for women, paying them while they learned to transform discarded tires into sandals. The small salaries we offered were meant to help subsidize the time it would take for each woman to hone her skill; we were providing opportunities for these women to learn something valuable, something sustainable. Once they had the skills, we would help them find work, either by selling their creations in the marketplace or by connecting them with local factories that could use their skills. As I thought about the women who would join our program, I felt a deep sense of hope. I truly believed that once they learned how to make sandals, they would have an income once again. They would rebuild their lives and pass that empowerment on to their families and communities.

Our sense of excitement and accomplishment didn't last long, however. The harsh reality of the economy quickly caught up with us. Haiti, a country already burdened by political instability and economic challenges, had few industries to speak of. Few goods were manufactured locally, which meant that even fewer employment opportunities existed for people who were looking to work. It wasn't just that education and job training were scarce; it was that the jobs themselves were simply not there, even for those who were educated or had skills. The unemployment rate in Haiti was staggering, hovering at nearly 70 percent. That number felt more like a weight than a statistic, and it was a stark reminder of the barriers we were up against. The poverty was layered, intricate, and deeply rooted. It felt like a cancer, slowly devouring any chance for skilled workers to make a living.

And yet I saw people living and pushing forward every single day. It was as if an invisible thread connected the small markets and informal jobs that kept the country's economy afloat, despite its many challenges. How did it all fit together? How did people manage to survive when formal jobs were so scarce? I couldn't pinpoint the ways but they were there, knitted into the fabric of everyday life. The invisible economy that sustained this city wasn't written down in books or taught in classrooms. It was something you learned by living it, by necessity, by sheer willpower. While I couldn't yet decode it, I knew it was my key. If I could understand how these unwritten systems worked, I could create something meaningful, a mechanism that didn't just teach skills but that tapped into the existing pulse of survival and made it stronger.

Over the next few months, I wandered in and out of the lanes of the downtown market, watching it rise from the rubble as merchants rebuilt their stalls. The streets were alive with the sounds of vendors calling out their wares and I felt the pulse of a dynamic city beginning to beat more steadily. It was in this busy city center that I met a man named Moncher. His voice carried the weight of struggle, yet he still found the strength to show me the realities of running a business in Haiti.

"Many of us operate in the shadows," he explained, gesturing to the movement around us. "My countrymen are forced to create an underground market, with a network of trust, where formal structures have failed us." I followed Moncher through the winding paths of the market, listening as he explained the invisible systems that kept life moving for so many Haitians. This was the shadow economy, a world of bartering and ingenuity, where vendors swapped goods without a single dollar changing hands—a bag of rice for a pile of mangoes, a bundle of clothing for a sack of charcoal.

Yet the shadow economy, while vital, didn't create opportunities for earning a real income or enjoying upward mobility. It was a cycle that provided just enough to get by but never enough to rise above. I thought about our sandal-training program and I realized that without formal businesses or steady demand, there would be nowhere for these women to work. There were no shoe companies to welcome our trained graduates. There wouldn't be customers with cash lining up around their stalls to buy their goods. Our efforts would only feed into the cycle of bartering, leaving them stuck in the same endless struggle.

We were going to train women in sandal-making and equip them with skills to escape poverty, and that was supposed to be enough. But it wasn't. The need was greater, the stakes higher. Then it struck me. I wasn't just going to be the trainer; I would have to open a business, become a salesperson, and lay the foundation of a new way forward. The idea scared me. I had never envisioned this path.

I sought counsel from Jolina. How could we create a system to fight poverty that would respectfully intertwine the deep-rooted norms of Haitian society? We both dreamed of an economically free Haiti where people had access to education, job training, and jobs, but did we really have to do it all ourselves? We realized that the conversations we had begun in her tent orphanage all those months ago had led us to this very moment. We decided then that if there were no factories to hire our trained women, we would build one ourselves.

By winter we had constructed not only a community center to facilitate our Elèv after-school program, but also a tiny sandal-making workshop in the middle of Port-au-Prince. Our workshop was pieced together from scraps of wood we found, pressed tightly up against the side of a concrete-block wall to form a makeshift lean-to. We stretched an old, faded blue tarp, one of those handed out by relief agencies, across the top to fashion a pitched roof. Rainwater would cascade down the sides, sparing the roof from collapse during Haiti's frequent downpours. The entire space was about the size of a typical Florida dining room, but every inch represented hope to us.

About a week after we constructed our sandal workshop, Jolina, Kim, and I sat on the floor with our three new Haitian teammates. Armed with razor blades, we began cutting discarded automobile tires into soles for what we envisioned as our African-inspired sandals. At first it felt exhilarating, turning trash into a useful, meaningful product. But we were in for a rude awakening. Tire rubber, we quickly discovered, is one of the most stubborn materials to work with. Each cut was a battle, the blades catching and slipping, our hands aching. And that was just the beginning. Sizing the sandals, sourcing the materials, designing a prototype, were all pieces of a puzzle we weren't quite sure how to solve.

Research and development became my new daily ritual, though "research" mostly meant trial and error. Lots and lots of error. My first design idea was bold: sandals made entirely from recycled car tires. The soles came from the sidewalls, while the straps were cut from repurposed inner tubes. We were thrilled when we finally made our first pairs. But our excitement faded as quickly as the sun rose. On the first hot afternoon we wore them, the inner tube straps heated up in the sun and burned the tops of our feet. Defeated but not deterred, I knew we had to find a better material for the straps. I just didn't know what.

Haiti, however, has a way of revealing solutions when you least expect them. Shortly after our first sandal prototype failed, I met a man in town who had a solution for us. He brought me to a small sunlit area in the heart of Port-au-Prince, where a group of women sat close together, quietly conversing and humming. Their hands danced across cords of cotton and hemp as they wove tiny knots into macramé

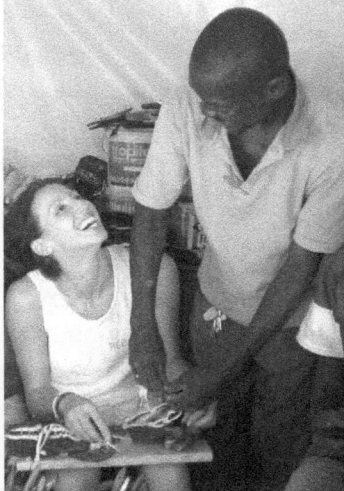

Port-au-Prince, 2010, the building of our first sandal workshop. It was a tiny lean-to made of scrap wood with an old tarp that hung over the edge, to try to protect us from the sun in the day and the rain at night.

projects. A skill passed down through generations, macramé is not typically used for sandal straps, but I could see this local artistry adding great value to our tire soles and I hired the group to make our straps for us.

Twelve months after the earthquake, we developed our second prototype sandal with tire soles and macramé straps. Admittedly, it was clunky, heavy, and less comfortable than we would have liked, but local relief workers and even some UN staff loved the concept and bought them anyway. The sales gave us a small sense of accomplishment, a glimmer of progress.

But just as we were finding our footing, the country landed on the brink of a new crisis when the Artibonite River became the epicenter of a deadly cholera outbreak. The river, which so many relied on for drinking, cooking, and bathing, had become infected when contaminated human waste from the United Nations peacekeeping force near Mirebalais leaked into it, bringing waterborne bacteria to thousands of Haitians. Sickness consumed different members of our team at any given time, but we were lucky. Even with the hospitals and cholera clinics constantly at maximum capacity, we always found a space and were given care. By the end of 2010, about 10,000 people had lost their lives to this terrible and preventable disease. I was so grateful that this time our small team was spared.

However, a disaster more personal to us was looming over our heads. We were out of cash. Every last dollar was gone, and all my credit cards were maxed out. I used to joke nervously, "Visa is our biggest sponsor; they just don't know it yet." But my mom didn't find the humor in it. She had a knack for reminding me that Visa bills were piling up back home, monthly tallies of the debt into which I was sinking. It didn't bother me, though, because in Haiti even the best credit couldn't buy food. Cash was king, and we didn't have any left. Kim and I made sure every penny went to our programs, leaving very little, and we could barely afford to buy food for ourselves. There were a few weeks when we ate only avocados and bags of tuna. Every day and night the same thing. For years after the earthquake, it would sicken me to walk down the tuna aisle at a grocery store. Each afternoon I would take out my pocketknife and cut the avocado in half, and we would sit on the floor and share it. Then our ritual was to smoke a cigarette to suppress our lingering hunger while we sipped a warm Coke. We became accustomed to this diet, but in other ways our struggles were changing me, and my moods began swinging from sad to angry without much warning.

My $7,000 and the money we had raised from the first charity event were long gone. We were surrounded by every need you could imagine, from education to reconstruction to housing to an economy that barely existed. We hadn't fleshed out how to operate both a charity and a business in Haiti, and we were losing stamina. Late in the year, Kim's husband returned home from his tour in Afghanistan, and Kim left Haiti to join him back in the United States. In that single moment, the fragile sense of partnership I had leaned on disappeared.

Now I was alone. Although I was making wonderful Haitian friends, my language skills were slow to develop, and my American accent made it tough for Haitians to understand me. Without a US counterpart to commiserate with, I was left to contend with my own thoughts.

CHAPTER 6

WHERE IT ALL STARTED

As you grow older, you will discover that you have two hands, one for helping yourself, the other for helping others.

Audrey Hepburn

o

Growing up, I was surrounded by love and support. My family was the kind that made you feel safe. But even with that security, something in me wasn't right. When I was just five years old, my mom noticed my strange relationship with food. I'd pick at meals or find excuses to avoid them altogether. It wasn't until years later, in my teens, that I was diagnosed as having an eating disorder, purging anorexia. Most days I starved myself, meticulously planning how to skip meals without raising suspicion. On the rare occasions I did eat, the guilt would overwhelm me and I'd purge. My disorder consumed every aspect of my life. At school, I'd sit in the courtyard pretending to eat while hiding the food I couldn't bring myself to swallow. Relationships became tangled in lies and avoidance because so much of life revolved around food.

Some days I couldn't tell where I ended and my eating disorder began. It was like a shadow, following me everywhere, consuming my thoughts and my identity. And it didn't hurt just me; it tore my family apart. My parents didn't understand why I wouldn't eat, but they were relentless in trying to save me. My mom tried everything. She cooked every meal with care, replacing fat and sugar with anything she thought I'd accept. She'd plate my food in tiny portions, spreading it thinly to make it look less daunting. She never gave up, even when I refused bite after bite.

When all else failed, my parents had no choice but to admit me to a hospital for children with eating disorders. I spent years going in and out of those places, rooms filled with whispers of shared pain and longing for freedom. Therapy, treatment plans, and counseling became the rhythm of my adolescence, but nothing seemed to work. In the end, what saved me wasn't a doctor, a diet, or even my family's love, though I clung to all those along the way. What saved me was learning to live a life filled with kindness and empathy for the world around me. That answer didn't come easily or immediately, but it was the only way I could begin to untangle myself from the disorder that had defined me for so long.

The evening I came to my realization is etched in my mind, as vivid as if it happened yesterday. My mom had made her famous lasagna, the kind she always whipped up when she wanted us all to sit down together as a family. I was determined to be "normal" that night. I was just going to eat, laugh, and maybe watch a movie after dinner. We gathered around our big marble dining table, my dad's pride and joy. I took slow, deliberate bites, trying to convince myself and everyone else that everything was fine. The taste of the rich, cheesy layers was both comforting and suffocating, each bite sitting like a stone in my belly. I finished as much as I could without drawing attention, careful not to overdo it.

Afterward, we wandered into the living room, my parents settling into their spots on the overstuffed old couch. I curled up beside them, sinking deep into its worn cushions. *Armageddon* came on the TV, one of my favorite movies. No matter how much I wanted to stay, to just exist in that moment with them, I couldn't. The food sat heavy in my stomach, screaming at me, taunting me. I slipped quietly off the couch and locked myself in the bathroom. I stood there for a long moment, staring at my reflection in the mirror. My face was flushed, and my eyes, filled with anger and shame, searched for answers I didn't have. I hated myself for not being able to stop this, for ruining what could have been a perfectly ordinary evening.

I turned on the shower to mask the sound, then leaned over the toilet. The ritual was the same one I had repeated countless times. But this time, it wasn't just dinner that came up. Blood streaked the bile, bright red and terrifying. Panic gripped me. Was it from my stomach? From my throat, raw and burning from years of abuse? I didn't know, but it didn't matter. My body was breaking down, betraying me, and I realized I couldn't keep living like this. I fell to my knees, tears streaming down my face, and begged God to help me. For the first time, I prayed with a desperation I'd never felt before. I swore that if He would take this terrible thing away from me, I would spend the rest of my life working to make the world a better place. In that tiny bathroom, surrounded by the sounds of running water and my own sobs, I begged for healing.

It was many years later, during the summer of 2003, that I finally found a reprieve, and in the most unexpected place, a busy street in South Africa. I was in the graduate program at the University of Central Florida and overheard some chatter about a group of sociology students heading to South Africa for a study abroad program. I wasn't a sociology major. I didn't have any friends on the trip or connections in South Africa. But none of that mattered. I felt a pull, a deep conviction that I needed to be in South Africa with this group. I knew it was a long shot, but I was determined to join them.

I tracked down the professor leading the trip, Dr. Kurtz, and requested a meeting. Sitting across from her in her cluttered office, I laid it all on the table, my background, my passion for exploring how societies work, and my newly burning desire to see South Africa. I spoke fast, trying to cram my enthusiasm into every word, but I could see her skepticism in the way she leaned back in her chair, arms crossed.

"You realize this is last-minute," she said, her voice firm. "The class is leaving in a few weeks. There's a lot of paperwork, and everything has to be expedited. It's up to you to get it all done in time."

"I'll handle it," I promised, leaning forward. "I'll take full responsibility."

Dr. Kurtz sighed and looked me over for a long moment. Then, to my relief, she nodded. "Fine. But if anything's incomplete, you're not getting on that plane."

I practically skipped out of her office, giddy at the thought of traveling to South Africa. But even as I started tackling the logistics, I wanted to be more than just a student, attending lectures at Cape Town University and taking guided tours. I wanted to live there, to work there, to immerse myself in the culture. Pushing my luck, I went back to Dr. Kurtz with my request. She raised an eyebrow but listened as I explained my desire for a deeper, more authentic experience. To my surprise, she didn't dismiss me outright. Maybe it was my persistence, or maybe it was her own South African roots that softened her resolve.

"I might know someone," she said, almost reluctantly. And just like that, things began to fall into place. Dr. Kurtz reached out to a longtime family friend in South Africa who offered me a job at St. Anne's Home, a refuge for women who had survived sexual violence and the children born from their trauma. She also arranged for me to stay with a host family, giving me the chance to live not as a tourist but as part of the community.

Our departure approached quickly, and in the blink of an eye my new sociology friends and I were standing at the airport, suitcases in hand. I said goodbye to my boyfriend and the comforts of home. After a string of layovers and a grueling sixteen-hour flight, we finally landed in Cape Town. The air was different, heavy with a mix of ocean breeze and something I couldn't yet name but later found out was the scent of wild fig trees, which often grow near the coast and give off a woody, slightly fruity aroma. That week, we dove headfirst into the city's cadence, soaking in its energy while grappling with its complex layers. Each weekday, we immersed ourselves in lectures at Cape Town University, uncovering the history and culture of South

Africa through the lens of apartheid. On weekends, we explored the beauty and contradictions of the city: its glittering coastline, its sprawling townships, and everything in between.

One weekend we joined the line of tourists waiting to ascend the famous flat-topped Table Mountain. The wait seemed endless, but the moment I stepped into the cable car and felt it rise, my breath caught. As we floated upward, the city stretched out below us, a collage of colors, shapes, and stories. At the summit, the view was extraordinary. Surrounded by the native wildlife and plants of the beautiful national park, I marveled at the Twelve Apostles Mountain Range in the distance. It was impossible not to feel a profound sense of privilege standing there, knowing that many of the local residents, those whose stories I had started to understand, would never have the means to experience this. I felt humbled, grateful, and heartbroken.

Before long, my classmates' time in Cape Town was winding down. This was the end of the journey for them, but for me it was just the beginning. Instead of heading to the airport, I boarded a bus bound for my host family's home near Khayelitsha, a township in the Western Cape. The ride should have been about an hour, but life had other plans. The bus broke down in the middle of nowhere, a barren stretch of road with nothing but silence and heat. Hours passed, the monotony broken only by the sound of the restless murmurs of the other passengers. I fell into a half-sleep until a new sound stirred me awake. A small crowd had gathered near the side of the road, their voices rising in curiosity. Drawn by the commotion, I stepped off the bus and walked closer.

Two men sat in the center of the group, carving into something with knives. It took me a moment to understand: they were slicing through old tires, transforming them into sandals right there on the roadside. What stood out most wasn't just the creativity of their work, but the way they were turning an ordinary, discarded object into something useful. Who could have guessed that on a broken-down bus outside Cape Town I'd find the spark for an idea that would one day start something beautiful in Haiti?

The bus finally sputtered back to life, and by the time we pulled into the station near my host family's home, night had fallen. Exhausted, I stepped off the bus, my body aching and my spirits low. But my host family greeted me with open arms, their warmth cutting through the weariness of the day. They certainly didn't have much, but what they had, they shared. Their generosity wasn't performative or reserved for the visiting stranger. It was a way of life, a deeply ingrained value that permeated every interaction. In their world, community wasn't an abstract concept; it was a state of being that was demonstrated through many small, selfless acts.

Once I was immersed in their family and community, I could see that food was hard to come by. But not on Thursday; every Thursday my host mother would find a way to prepare a pot of soup for anyone in the area who needed a meal. The ingredients were whatever she could harvest from her small garden or what her neighbors brought her. Everyone knew of her kindness, and by evening the aroma of spice wafting in the air would draw the community in. My host mother stood over large metal vats, ladling bowl after bowl with a serene smile, and there was always just enough for everyone who came to her doorstep.

I was not the only one moved by her spirit of generosity, as evidenced on her sixtieth birthday. That morning our house buzzed with activity. My host sisters laid out their best dresses, carefully pressing the fabric with hands practiced in making the most out of little. My host mother, modest as ever, waved off the attention and went about her tasks, but I noticed a little twinkle of anticipation in her eyes. By afternoon we were all dressed in our finest clothes, and we made the short hike to the community center in the middle of town. The family was seated at a large table at the end of the room, a position of honor. I held my cup of the sweet tea that was served, unsure of what to expect as the first guest, a child no more than seven years old, stood to speak.

Clutching a worn old bible with trembling hands, she read a verse. Following her lead, other community members came forward. Some recited poems, their words flowing with emotion. Others spoke plainly, sharing personal stories of how my host mother had touched their lives.

"When my son was sick, you brought us soup," one woman said, her voice cracking. "You never asked for anything in return." Another man spoke of her laughter, how it filled the neighborhood on even the hardest days. As the day went on, I watched my host mother grow taller and taller. Her children beamed with pride, her husband sat a little straighter, and even I felt like I was part of something larger, something sacred. This celebration taught me what binds people together, and I never wanted to celebrate a birthday the same way again. I wanted all the special occasions in my life to feel as intentional and honest as they felt this day.

My work in South Africa took place in the nearby town of Woodstock. As I walked through the gates to enter St. Anne's Home, a place where the air felt heavy with both sorrow and resilience, I was consumed with anticipation. This was a refuge for women who had endured unspeakable violence, and many carried babies born from their attacks. The home provided them and their children not only shelter but a chance to start over. Since I had studied dance art therapy as an undergraduate, my role was to hold dance classes that would help the women process their trauma. I stepped into the modest room, its walls lined with yoga mats and mirrors. The women shuffled in hesitantly, eyes downcast, shoulders tight, their wounds etched into every movement. I introduced myself and explained that dance therapy was about reconnecting with the body, about using movement and creativity to express what words often couldn't. Even as I spoke I realized that I would learn far more about healing and survival from these women than I could ever teach them.

South Africa taught me many things, including hunger that wasn't self-inflicted, the relentless, gnawing emptiness that comes when there's truly nothing to eat. Long periods would stretch with very little food, and this time it wasn't my choice. Hunger from want was a stark reminder of how fragile life could be when something I always took for granted was out of my control. During those desperate times, and through the bravery of the women at St. Anne's, I found my own healing, too. I learned to value not just the food that was available, but the body that carried me through the struggle. Every meal became a symbol of survival, a gift not to be taken for granted. Around me, the haunting reality of hundreds, sometimes thousands, of people enduring the same agony unfolded daily. They waited and hoped, often without relief. It was there, in that crucible of despair, that I was healed, and I made a silent vow: never to disrespect my food again. To waste nothing. To honor the hands that grow, prepare, and serve it. And to remember always that food is more than sustenance; it's life.

Overcoming my eating disorder gave me a second chance. With it, the vow I made to God in my parents' bathroom became my compass, guiding me toward a life dedicated to fighting for social justice and the rights of the most vulnerable. That path would sometimes lead me into unexpected places—some full of beauty, others uncharted and dangerous territory—and ultimately into the heart of Haiti's catastrophic earthquake, where I emerged physically unscathed but would ultimately be thrashed and tested emotionally.

CHAPTER 7

FINDING MY PLACE

○

I hadn't realized how much Kim's departure affected me. The small team I started with had slowly dispersed over time and the loneliness was consuming me, bringing me to a dark place emotionally. Every moment I slept safely behind our compound walls, every small comfort I allowed myself felt like a betrayal to the Haitians, who were the ones really suffering. Just outside the walls people were starving, grieving, enduring pain in ways I could never fully comprehend. The guilt was gnawing at me. I ramped up the number of cigarettes I smoked to dull the anxiety that penetrated my thoughts, but this new personality I developed was unfamiliar, especially to anyone who knew me back home. I became hollow and distant, withdrawing from everything in my life in the States. I was especially drifting from the one person I should have been clinging to most, my fiancé Noah. I didn't know how to talk to him, my family, or my friends anymore. Haiti was transforming me, but not in the ways I had imagined when I first arrived. It was breaking me apart, piece by piece, forcing me to confront dark parts of myself I didn't even know existed.

In the depths of my struggles, the only person I did confide in was Dr. Swanson, my pastor at First Presbyterian Church of Orlando (FPCO). He became my sounding board, the one person to whom I could lament about the never-ending shortages of food and money. He let me swear and spew angrily in emails expressing my frustration that there was never enough help or supplies. I was running on empty, and every word I typed was a desperate attempt to make sense of the havoc around and inside me. The biggest surprise about finding a confidant in Dr. Swanson was that my despair was rooted in my feeling abandoned by God.

I was convinced this was unchristian of me, a betrayal of the faith I was supposed to hold onto. My family was already worried about me, and I didn't want to burden them with the weight of my unraveling faith. Sharing it with others in my church community felt impossible. My liberal views often clashed with the more traditional beliefs around me, leaving me feeling like I didn't belong. But Dr. Swanson didn't judge me or tell me what I should feel. Instead he listened, offering kindness without conditions. Those emails transcended pastoral guidance. They were threads of hope I clung to, each word a reminder that I wasn't facing the brokenness of this complicated situation alone.

When I returned to the United States for short fundraising trips or to sell our sandals, I could wear a mask of normality just long enough to rally the support we desperately needed for our work. But my behavior was spiraling out of control, and behind closed doors the cracks were impossible to conceal. My emotions swung between dark anger and a deep sadness accompanied by uncontrollable sobbing. I developed a quick and mean tongue, and I didn't hesitate to unleash it on anyone who dared complain about the price of a Starbucks coffee or a gallon of gas, or some other trivial discomfort of life in the developed world. My outrage felt righteous in the moment, but deep down I knew it was misplaced. Noah bore the brunt of this anger. It was unfair, but I couldn't control it. I continued to smoke, which disgusted him, and my crying spells seemed to come out of nowhere and last for way too long, confusing and upsetting him.

Eventually Dr. Swanson helped me find my faith again and dispel all the lies I was telling myself. My heart softened so I could focus on my work in Haiti, but not before Noah and I both realized we wouldn't make it. I had seen too much and changed too much. I was no longer the person Noah had fallen in love with, and the path I was determined to follow would no longer suit the married life we had been planning. Even after we parted ways, Noah continued to support me and our work in Haiti as a great friend, but the life I had created in the States seemed to be over. Haiti changed me for better and for worse, and there was no going back.

The real relief I craved, partnership in Haiti, came when I least expected it. On May 30, 2011, one of REBUILD's first and most dedicated volunteers, Sandra, kept a promise she had made a year earlier, to move to Haiti after college graduation and work with me. True to her word, on receiving her diploma from New York University, she packed her bags and took the leap of faith. I had met Sandra years earlier in Orlando, back when REBUILD was just an idea taking

Spring 2011, Rue Pelican, Delmas, Haiti. The REBUILD globally compound was first established behind the razor-walled gate. During their daily walks Sandra and Boot navigated trash rivers and flooding streets but were always greeted by stray dogs.

shape. Even then, she was extraordinary—sharp, driven, and unshakable. When I needed help organizing our very first charity event, Sandra was there, sleeves rolled up, ready to make things happen. But it wasn't until she visited Haiti in August 2010 that I had truly seen her heart.

Her first trip took place during a two-week school break. Wide-eyed but determined, she didn't just *see* the rubble-strewn streets or the challenges we faced; she *felt* them. It was as though the weight of the place settled on her shoulders, and instead of buckling, she carried it. I watched her absorb everything, our struggles, our heartbreak, and the hope that kept us going. When she returned to New York to finish school, I wondered whether her resolve would waver. But it didn't. Instead, she stayed connected, committed, and quietly supportive from a distance. And now she was here.

Sandra couldn't have come at a more critical time and she got straight to work, taking up where Kim had left off and focusing on our Elèv program. Her passion for REBUILD was no longer theoretical; it was personal. She experienced firsthand the choices we faced daily, some so harrowing that we never spoke of them in charity updates or on social media. Everywhere we went street children begged us for help. They wanted to go to school, but even if we paid for them to do so, they faced problems and challenges that school couldn't address. How would they get their next meal? Where would they sleep? How could they stay safe living on the streets?

Sandra and I wrestled with these questions every day and made decisions that felt impossible. With our limited resources, we were choosing which children to help, knowing we couldn't help them all. However, having her by my side brought a renewed sense of strength. She constantly reminded me that while we couldn't fix everything, what we *could* do still mattered, and it was important to commit only to goals we could see through.

We committed to never making a promise we couldn't keep or start a project we couldn't finish. The children, still so young, had endured more broken promises in their short lives than anyone should, and I refused to be another person who let them down. Starting small and being intentional with each child was not just our best option; it was our only option. The promises we made weren't mere words; they were commitments. And with each one, I carried the weight of knowing that for these children, trust wasn't given freely; it was earned, slowly and carefully, one fulfilled promise at a time.

Later that year my life intersected with Rony, a proud and talented thirteen-year-old bracelet maker who would in time become the living proof that our model of development did what we hoped, help educate young people and then put them on a career path. Rony's mother and four sisters depended on him, and he exuded a maturity that came from growing up surrounded by strong female energy. He first heard about REBUILD globally and me from a local man who suggested I would be a good paying customer, and Rony should try to sell me his bracelets.

Being the young and resourceful entrepreneur he was, Rony learned my name and made a macramé bracelet that spelled it out. Well, almost. The white plastic beads spelled out J-U-L-L-Y in black ink, a small but endearing mistake. Rony presented the bracelet to me with a wide, hopeful smile. The gesture moved me, and I called my teammates over to admire Rony's work. Trying to support his bracelet-making business in the best way I could at that moment, I told Rony I would buy one for each of my colleagues. He was thrilled with the order. Every night after school he worked diligently on the bracelets, and the following Thursday he returned to our workshop with them. Each bracelet was precisely and beautifully made. We all immediately saw the talent and the promise Rony had. Even at his young age, there was something notable about him, and you could almost see the future in his face.

Sandra and I were just about to kick off the next year of our Elèv program, and we had enough money for ten more student scholarships. By now, the program was established to not only pay school tuition and after-school tutoring, but we also arranged fun weekend activities. We had one spot left, and I couldn't help but think it was meant for Rony. Buying his bracelets was a nice gesture, but including him in the Èlev program could make a much more substantial difference in his education. A day later I extended the offer and asked Rony to join our program. He politely declined, explaining that his mother didn't trust foreigners. To her, foreigners in Haiti were exploiters, coming to take advantage of the local people, profit from their hardships, and then leave. Even though it stung a little, I knew enough about the problems with outsiders in Haiti and understood her hesitation. Rony continued making his bracelets and watching me from a distance.

One Sunday afternoon Rony stumbled upon a post I had shared on Facebook. We were having a swim party with a group of street kids at a local hotel that allowed us to use the pool one afternoon a week. Here the kids got to be just kids, swimming, playing, and eating a lunch made just for them. Rony admitted the post had a profound impact on him.

"I've never seen a *blan* (white person) love street kids like this before," he told me. He thought it was "cool," but his mother wasn't impressed. I could tell from Rony's recounting of their conversation that her voice was layered with mistrust.

"Ah, it will only last a few days," she had told him with finality. "They'll use you to make money and then tell you to leave. Just wait and see." Those words lingered in his mind, but he wanted to believe I was different. He carried his mother's skepticism like a shield, but against her wishes, he decided he would accept the scholarship I had offered him.

When our ten new students showed up for orientation at REBUILD globally, I explained the expectations. The students lived in three different tent camps, each attending their local school. They were to do well in their classes and serve as role models for the other students. In return their tuition would be covered, and we would offer special Saturday activities and extra help to their families on an "as needed" basis. Rony listened with a mixture of hesitation and curiosity, like someone who had been let down too many times but still clung to the faintest hope that just maybe this time would be different. Gathering the students around, I announced our first activity, trying to inject excitement into my voice.

"Tomorrow, I need you all to wear your nicest clothes," I said with a smile. "We're going to take pictures for the

REBUILD globally yearbook." The room filled with murmurs of surprise, but Rony just stared at me. In his world foreigners took pictures of kids only when they were dirty and looked desperate, images meant to tug at heartstrings and open wallets. But to take pictures when they were looking their best? To showcase their pride and dignity? That was something entirely new to him. For the first time, doubt crept into his shield of mistrust. Rony started to wonder whether Sandra and I really were different. Maybe we weren't just another pair of well-meaning visitors who would take pictures, raise money, and then disappear. Maybe we genuinely wanted to see him succeed.

The school year was touch-and-go, and I was certainly still finding my footing. Every day was a balancing act, with us learning how to navigate challenges, connect with students and their teachers, and piece together how we could best support the children's education and the schools they attended. But just as I started to feel like I was gaining ground, the end of the year brought something unexpected. Some of Rony's classmates didn't pass the national exam. I was baffled. The kids wanted to be in school, they were determined and motivated, and their teachers told me they were giving it their all. So what was holding them back?

I needed answers, so I began spending more time with the students in their classrooms. What I discovered was both frustrating and shocking. Classes were taught in Creole, the language of the children's homes, their streets, their lives. But the national exams? They were written in French. One of Haiti's two official languages, French wasn't just a tool for communication; it was a symbol of privilege, the language of the elite spoken fluently by only a select few. And here were our students, expected to pass critical exams written in a language they barely understood. It was like asking them to run a marathon on crutches. Determined to bridge the language gap, we hired a French tutor, and our Saturday program became a French language lab. Down the road, as we learned more about the challenges in the students' comprehension, we added additional labs in English, math, social science, and chemistry to support classroom work.

The next year, every single student in our program passed the national exams. It was extraordinary. The input, patience, and determination of Rony and his classmates shaped an education model that didn't just work but made a significant impact. Together, we proved a powerful truth: we didn't need to isolate ourselves from the community. Instead, we could strengthen what already existed by filling in the gaps, supporting local schools and addressing their challenges. As another benefit of our program, paying tuition for our students on time had profound effects. Often unpaid for months in the past, teachers now received their salaries on schedule. They arrived in classrooms ready to teach, motivated, and prepared. This didn't just support the students in our program; the school principals told us that REBUILD globally elevated the entire classroom experience for all their students.

Rony taught me more than I ever expected, not just about his own life but about the deeper dynamics between Haitians and foreigners. His honesty shaped the way I spent my days thereafter. At the time, I was still supporting a few orphanages. It wasn't part of any official REBUILD globally initiative but something I had carried over from the relationships I had built after the earthquake. I hadn't yet grasped the complexities of these institutions, and the time I was dedicating to them began to pull me away from the students in our Elèv program and the women in our sandal workshop. I felt torn. How could I just walk away when these orphanages were so vulnerable? But I was beginning to realize a hard truth: my presence alone might have been doing more harm than good.

For Haitians, caring for orphaned children is deeply rooted in cultural values. It's an extension of community and family, a shared responsibility. For many foreigners, though, it often starts as an emotional response to visible suffering: an impulse to fix what appears broken. At first glance such aid seems noble. But I began to notice how those differences in approach affected the children. When Jolina opened an orphanage in her own community, she understood the struggles of growing up in Haiti and had a personal connection to the children in her care. The children in her orphanage wouldn't face the pain of abandonment because Jolina would be a constant presence.

In contrast, I saw many well-meaning foreigners driven by love and compassion open orphanages, too. But the heartbreaking reality was that most of them were in Haiti only temporarily. What started as a refuge for children often became yet another source of loss and instability when the founders left. I saw the cycle unfold again and again: the children would bond with these temporary caretakers, only to face the pain of abandonment when the projects dissolved. The damage done by those abandoned orphanages is still being felt in their communities today. It was a sobering realization for me, one that forced me to rethink my priorities and my role in the community.

When I first heard the word *orphan,* I automatically equated it with the loss of parents. But in Haiti and other places of poverty, that isn't always the case. Many of the "orphans" I met still had parents, parents who, in sheer desperation, brought their children to foreign-run orphanages in hopes of giving them a better life. The promise of regular meals, the chance to attend school, and the possibility of escaping poverty drove them to make heart-wrenching decisions. These children weren't true orphans; they were poverty orphans, separated from their families not by death but by destitution.

Too often, these systems bred opportunists who saw the orphanage as a profitable venture. Managing these intended refuges would become less about providing a home for children and more about exploiting their circumstances. Families continued to hand over their children, believing it was their only option and unaware of the cycle of neglect and greed that had taken root. It was a harsh and humbling lesson about the unintended consequences of our efforts, and the critical importance of working within and respecting the existing cultural framework.

I made a promise to myself that my story in Haiti wouldn't end in abandonment or fleeting efforts. I would work with Jolina and the team to create opportunities, not dependencies. To stay true to my newfound belief that love and good intentions were not enough, I committed to stop working on projects that didn't align with our mission, and to fully focus on the long-term outcome. Sustainability, cultural understanding, and a commitment to the long haul were essential. Whatever we built, a program, a business, or a partnership, we wanted it to endure not just for a season but for generations.

Even as we continued refining our program's execution, with the new graduation success I was growing more confident in the Elèv program. The foundation felt solid, and it seemed we had the right people in the right places. Now it was time to shift my focus back to the women in the sandal training program. Transforming our existing structure from a nonprofit sandal-training program to an actual sandal business would be handled with the same care and intention as was taken to create REBUILD globally. This company would be a place that didn't just create jobs but also supported career development, focusing on the people and not just profit. The tiny workshop we had already established, although far from glamorous, embodied the foundation of a *social enterprise*, a term new to my vocabulary but powerful in its intentions. At this early stage in our company's development we were still just four women from the neighborhood learning to make sandals from tires, but I could see a bigger future. We wouldn't be just a short-term fix for a few women; the need was too great. This social enterprise would someday embody all our values and become a beacon of hope and opportunity. We would call our company Deux Mains, "two hands" in French, as a reminder that everything we wanted to achieve would be built with our own hands.

One day, I promised, we'd turn this little training center into a huge factory and our goods would be sold globally. It was an audacious dream, especially in the poorest country

Summer 2012, REBUILD campus, Port-au-Prince, Haiti. REBUILD globally students are involved in a variety of programs that enhance their learning from computer classes to language and leadership classes.

in the Western Hemisphere. And I was terrified. Starting a business anywhere is risky, but doing it in Haiti felt like balancing on a razor's edge. The stakes couldn't have been higher. These weren't just numbers on a spreadsheet or ideas in a pitch deck; these were people's lives. Failure wasn't an option. I had to get it right, not just for the women in the workshop or the students in the classrooms, but for myself.

CHAPTER 8

LOVE IN A HOPELESS PLACE

> I loved watching you bumble around the carnage of PAP, searching for a way to help people. It was something I had not seen with true passion before! You gave me hope in humanity.
>
> *Mark Billy Billingham*

○

Moving to Haiti marked the beginning of a new chapter in my life, but it was far from what I expected. Since I'd arrived, my engagement to Noah had failed, leaving me heartbroken, and the weight of running a charity while working to build a sandal business grew daily. Romance was the farthest thing from my mind, but life has a way of surprising us. I never imagined that on a cracked and littered road inside Log Base I'd cross paths with the man I would one day marry. But that is in fact where I first laid eyes on Billy, a British man with the assured confidence born of a lifetime of service.

Billy had joined the military at the age of seventeen, spending most of his adult life serving his country. When the earthquake hit Haiti, he was halfway across the world in Iraq, running a security company he had built with a friend from the Special Forces, the elite UK miliary unit to which he had belonged. The news of the disaster hit him hard, and he couldn't shake the images of suffering and destruction that filled his television screen. It didn't take long for him to realize he needed to do something to help. A man of quick action, he decided not to wait for the Port-au-Prince airport to sort itself out. Instead he booked a flight to the Dominican Republic on the neighboring side of the island, rented a car, and drove right to the center of the disaster zone.

Billy was mysterious, his confidence intoxicating, and his British accent irresistible. I knew from the moment we met there was something very special about him. He was unmistakable, too, always wearing a pair of sand-colored shorts and dark, dusty boots, with his backpack hanging off his right shoulder. We were both living at the UN base, but since he was a military man, with the right credentials to live there, he was legal. He pitched his small tent in the center of the compound, a stark reflection of his straightforward, no-frills nature. It was utilitarian, no pretenses, no fuss.

The expat community grew smaller as time went on, and it was inevitable that any volunteers who remained in Haiti would eventually meet, given how few places existed for foreigners to relax and unwind. Thus, after our initial meeting our paths crossed often. We also found ourselves at the same meetings hosted by the United Nations. Often Billy and I stood at the back of the room, exchanging glances as frustrations ran high. The meetings were followed by nightly rendezvous at the same hangout places everyone frequented, to drink local rum or Prestige and lament about the messes of the day. We were all deeply focused on our missions, but there was a quiet pull between the two of us that made me think we would become friends.

Yet Billy kept his distance in those early days. He was an enigma, polite but reserved. He avoided eye contact and ignored me in group conversations, directing his focus elsewhere. While he seemed to effortlessly strike up friendships with Kim and Malia, I felt invisible in his presence. Money was tight for us, so Kim, Malia, and I decided to pool our resources and buy a single, battered Nokia flip phone to share. It became our lifeline in a world of limited communication. Billy knew we shared the phone, yet whenever he texted, he'd address Kim or Malia by name, never me. Each message he sent felt like a deliberate omission, a subtle way of reinforcing my suspicion: Billy simply didn't like me.

Then one night a year later, a friend invited us all to an art gallery opening in Pètion-Ville, and that illusion was shattered. As I excitedly bathed and put on a dress, an extremely rare occurrence, my mind raced with the anticipation of soaking in the art and mountain atmosphere, very different from the lower lands of Tabarre where we lived. It had been months since I had experienced a cultural event like this, and we intended to make a night of it. So did Billy, apparently. He showed up, and not in the way I expected. It didn't take him long to indulge in too many beers, followed by a few reckless tequila shots. His usual calm and distant demeanor seemed to evaporate as the night wore on.

I was admiring a giant bear statue tucked into the corner of the gallery when he approached, his steps unsteady, his face flushed. Before I could say anything, he cornered me, his eyes wide with a mix of nerves and tequila-induced boldness.

"You make me nervous," he blurted out, stumbling over his words. I froze, caught completely off guard. And then, with the kind of candor only alcohol could summon, he dropped the bombshell: "And I'm in love with you." For a moment, the murmur of conversations, the clinking of glasses, the distant strains of music, all faded away. All I could hear was the pounding of my heart and the unfiltered truth in his voice. The man who had kept his distance, avoided eye contact, and ignored me for months had just upended everything I thought I knew.

After the art gallery event was over, I though Billy's tequila-fueled confession would be history too, but he didn't let it go. He texted that phone more than 50 times that night, professing his love. Knowing the effects of alcohol, I just laughed it off and pretended nothing had happened. After all, we were practically strangers. Billy seemingly agreed, and we both silently decided to just ignore that exchange.

But as the days turned into weeks, and the weeks into months, Billy kept showing up, always willing to help and never demanding anything in return. One day, our little group decided to go to Leogane, the area where Josh had originally helped build tent camps many months before. A new camp-building project was underway, and the organizers needed support. Our backpacks were packed and our plan in place, but that morning I came down with another stomach bug.

Billy got word that I was ill and decided to stay behind as well. That afternoon he and his driver Danny showed up to check on me. Billy knew of a hotel in Pétion-Ville where I could get pumpkin soup, a local Haitian delicacy, and he thought it would be good for me. I climbed into the backseat of the car with him, and Danny drove us up the mountain. The city outside the window was still a jarring mix of beauty and chaos, debris-strewn streets, makeshift tents, and piles of rubble that spoke of the earthquake's wrath. But as we ascended into Pétion-Ville, the scenery began to change. We parked the car in a spot that overlooked the city. The air was cooler here, and the landscape seemed untouched by the destruction below. I found myself walking along a perfectly manicured path lined with colorful trees and lush gardens, beauty that felt out of place.

Once we passed the glamorous staircase inside the hotel and went out the other side, a huge glistening pool and a restaurant that sat in the trees awaited us. I was stunned that places like this were still open, but the hotel had suffered very little damage from the earthquake. Everything about it felt surreal, like a dream I wasn't entirely sure I belonged in. Billy led me to a table shaded by a canopy of branches, and soon enough, a steaming bowl of pumpkin soup was set before me. I took a sip, and my stomach felt at ease. But as the meal went on, I couldn't help but notice that Billy kept glancing at his watch. At first I ignored it, but eventually curiosity got the better of me.

"Do you have somewhere else to be?" I asked, trying to mask my irritation with a half-smile. Billy looked up at me, his face softening into a grin.

"No," he said. "But you do." I blinked, confused, but he didn't offer an explanation.

After we finished our lunch, he led me to another staircase and down. My curiosity was piqued as I trailed behind him through the winding corridors of the hotel. When we emerged into a tranquil, softly lit spa, my jaw dropped open.

"What are we doing here?" I asked, the confusion evident in my voice.

Billy turned to me with that signature grin of his and simply said, "You're getting a pedicure." I stared at him, speechless. A pedicure? I hadn't even bathed properly in days, let alone given any thought to the condition of my feet. I opened my mouth to protest, but he was already guiding me to the check-in counter, where I heard the receptionist confirm the appointment.

"Julie Smith," she said, glancing at the logbook.

"Smith?" I whispered to him, raising an eyebrow. Billy shrugged nonchalantly.

"I didn't know your last name," he admitted, his voice tinged with humor. "So I guessed." I couldn't help but laugh at the absurdity of it all. Julie Smith. It sounded so ordinary, so far removed from the life I was living. But as I sat down in the spa chair, the luxury of being pampered began to sink in. I was full of mixed emotions. Conscious of my fragile, newly single state, I just kept telling myself, *No matter what, do not fall for this man.* But the walls I had built around my heart were already crumbling.

After my pedicure we climbed back in the car and spent the next few hours driving around Pétion-Ville. As we wove through the streets, I was struck by how different this part of Haiti felt. Unlike the areas of devastation to which I had grown accustomed in Tabarre, this place seemed to hold a semblance of normalcy.

I didn't reflect for long, because there wasn't a moment of silence between us. Billy opened up about his life, and his years in the British Special Forces when he put himself in crazy amounts of danger. He spoke about the SAS, where he had spent the last years of his military career. At first I couldn't fully grasp what he was saying.

"SAS?" I asked, tilting my head in confusion. He chuckled.

"It's a branch of the British Special Forces," he explained, his tone modest, almost dismissive. I had no idea what this was, or how elite a soldier he had been. I was a pacifist at heart and had always surrounded myself with people who were like me. Billy was my exact opposite. Yet I couldn't look away as he described his time in the SAS—the danger, the camaraderie, the discipline it took to thrive in such an elite force. He told his stories with a mix of humor and gravity, painting vivid pictures of moments I could barely imagine. Somehow, amid the adrenaline-laced narratives, I began to see something deeper. Billy wasn't just a soldier; he was a man who had faced the edges of human experience and come out the other side. It wasn't just bravery he epitomized; it was humanity.

Billy was older than I, and I knew he had seen far more of life than I had. But somehow working in a disaster zone had put us all on a parallel plane. Our lives back home felt a million miles away, and our differences faded. The only thing that mattered was the work we were doing at that moment.

As I spent more time with Billy, I realized he wasn't in Haiti just to help temporarily; he had a vision. He was spearheading a project as ambitious as it was inspiring. His original plan was to donate prefabricated buildings and build a hospital. Prefab buildings were an ideal solution in a post-disaster landscape, since they came packed with everything needed to make them operational and could be assembled in record time. They also required lots of local labor. From past experiences, Billy knew nothing would help Haitians recover more quickly than getting trained in this construction method and having a paycheck in their hands. His commitment to empowering others mirrored my own, and I couldn't help but admire him for it.

Poorly coordinated efforts and the continued mayhem of the time made executing anything extremely difficult. As happened with many other projects, things changed, and the hospital was not the first building Billy commissioned for construction. Instead, a chance meeting with his friend Sean Penn, who was taking a break from his acting career to help with the recovery efforts, gave Billy an opportunity to donate his prefabs to the charity Sean was creating.

Sean's nonprofit, JPHRO, had become one of the most visible organizations in Haiti after the earthquake. At this time, it had transformed Haiti's most elite golf course, Pétion-Ville Club, into a camp for more than 50,000 families. A city of tents stood where luxury had once reigned, overlooking the entire city. Together, a Hollywood icon and an SAS soldier were able to quickly and efficiently accomplish what had seemed impossible. Within the camp, they established a functioning school and a women's clinic, bringing a glimmer of hope to those who had endured so much.

As he and Sean were working on this project, Billy uncovered another great need—for better housing for relief workers in Tabarre. The accommodations we had pieced together for ourselves were wearing us down. Living in tents made sleep a rare luxury, and peeing in the streets was normal. I realize how privileged I am to complain about this, but not having electricity for months on end was soul-crushing. We couldn't flick on a light switch to do something as simple as finding our phone. And I never really appreciated the ease of turning on a tap of running water to brush my teeth or flush the toilet until that was no longer available. The experience was sucking the life from us.

Billy used his knowledge of building military camps in the Middle East to create something similar in the middle of Port-au-Prince. His vision was bold: a hotel in the heart of a shattered city. While most saw adversity, Billy saw opportunity, and not for personal gain but for the comfort of the people dedicated to helping Haiti. He knew the relief workers, already burning out from months of backbreaking work and grueling conditions, needed a place to recharge. At the same time, he saw an urgent need to provide jobs and rebuild the economy. And so the Caribbean Lodge was born. Thanks to Billy's foresight and his passion for getting income back into the pockets of survivors, his hotel became a haven for hundreds of people for years to come.

I will never forget my first night at the Caribbean Lodge. At the time, it wasn't the polished refuge it would later become, but rather a rough construction site known around town as "Billy's compound." My friend Kevin was invited to a barbecue Billy was hosting and casually suggested I should tag along. Kevin didn't know about the tequila-fueled confession at the art gallery, the pedicure in Pétion-Ville, or the butterflies I had struggled to suppress ever since. He only figured that Billy and I might have a few mutual acquaintances.

Barbecues in those days weren't exactly gourmet affairs. The menu was sausage, which I could never bring myself to eat. But no one ever passes up the opportunity to unwind with comrades after another punishing day of work. So I didn't hesitate to accept Kevin's invitation. Secretly eager to see Billy again, I hopped on the back of Kevin's red Suzuki motorbike, and we headed down the debris-strewn streets, the familiar sights of tent clusters and crumbling buildings blurring in the headlights. The closer we got to Billy's compound, the louder my heart pounded.

That night didn't seem to end for Billy and me. We talked until the first rays of sunlight started creeping over the horizon. Billy had a way of bringing out the best in me, the parts I had buried under exhaustion and the endless grind of relief work. I even picked up a guitar, my fingers instinctively finding chords I hadn't played in years. When I finally did crawl into bed, it wasn't in the suffocating confines of my old tent. Instead, I spent the night in one of Billy's forty-foot metal shipping containers. It was such an upgrade. The next morning at breakfast I thanked Billy for the restful night of sleep. He looked at me in disbelief when I mentioned I was still living in a tent camp.

"You're kidding me," he said, shaking his head. "You're moving into a shipping container. Today." And that was it. Kevin rode his motorbike home alone and I never slept in that miserable tent again.

I was thrilled to upgrade my living situation. The paint on the shipping container was chipping everywhere, and as

Summer 2011/2012, Billy's Compound, Port-au-Prince, Haiti. Billy and I hashed out each day's extreme events, from BBQ's to dinners at the US Embassy. We were acutely aware that anyone outside our small circle of friends would never believe the things we were experiencing, nor the dichotomy of the country.

the sun rose in the mornings, the heat would penetrate the metal sides, turning the interior into an oven. If I accidentally rolled over and touched the wall with my bare skin, I'd wake up with a searing reminder of the heat. But none of that mattered. It was paradise. For the first time in a long time, I had access to generator power. There were switches that, with a flick of my wrist, gave me light, and there were two metal bars that locked the doors of my new home. The containers were even segregated, with pieces of plywood to create bedrooms.

It wasn't just the physical building that buoyed my spirits; it was the relationships I was making as well. We all seemed to cling to each other, drawn by the challenges we faced and the shared drive to make a difference. Billy and I, especially, grew closer. We would spend hours late into the evening discussing poverty, the dire state of the orphanages in Haiti, and our dreams for our work there. He always had his eye on me, and although I can take care of myself and didn't feel I needed any sort of help or protection, that extra layer of security gave me an added boost of courage. Soon we became the best of friends and eventually combined our work and projects so we could join forces. We were better together, finding strength in each other. Moving into Billy's compound was a turning point, and the beginning of many great things we would do together.

As he oversaw every detail of his hotel-building project, Billy stayed mostly inside the compound. I, however, was out in the field every day, meeting and talking with local people. Each day brought new stories, tales of loss, resilience, and determination. Understanding hearts and minds was important to Billy, and he trusted me to be a bridge. My conversations with others outside the walls of the hotel helped him and his team understand the deeper needs of the people they were working among. It wasn't long before he allowed me to coordinate all his community donations. Because he was building the hotel, he had access to valuable resources like bunk beds and water filters that we could distribute to organizations we trusted.

My living conditions were dramatically improving, and so was the quality of my life with this new opportunity. However, the growing costs of running my charity and sandal business were becoming impossible to sustain. The numbers didn't add up, and I could feel bankruptcy creeping closer with every passing day. It wasn't just frustrating—it was terrifying. I needed to find a way to bring in money, fast. Then an idea took hold of me. I had a skill I could lean on. Long before I worked at United Way, I had studied dance and choreography as an undergraduate. I had even built a career out of dancing once. Now was the time; I could go back to my roots and do it again.

I had always cherished the way dance can heal both bodies and minds. Back in Miami, my mornings in college had started in the ballet studio, where I worked hard to make up for the years I hadn't trained as a kid. Somehow I turned that late start into a real career. My first job out of college was for a company called New Vision Cirque, where I performed as a dancer. Not long after being hired, I was also trained as an aerialist and spent many years on stage as a dancer and aerial silks performer. I had imagined that that part of my life was now in the past, but the company had always supported

Summer 2011, Billy's Compound, Port-au-Prince, Haiti. Hanging fifteen feet in the air by a crane I was able to practice my cirque routines, preparing to perform in the States and abroad to earn money for our work in Haiti.

my nontraditional life decisions and was happy to offer me a spot back in the show if I could relearn the routines.

All I had to do now was summon the physical and mental strength to climb a silk chiffon rope thirty feet into the air and hang gracefully from one arm, in the middle of Haiti. I had a lot of training to do to prepare to perform again, but I knew I could do it and Billy was determined to support me. He made sure I had everything I needed to train. Each night after work, Billy arranged for the crane driver to hang my silk chiffon from the crane so I could practice my routines. Not only was I able to work for New Vision Cirque when it toured and make much-needed cash for REBUILD globally and Deux Mains, but I also ended up performing quite a bit in Haiti, even for the hotel guests on the opening night of the Caribbean Lodge.

New Vision Cirque continued to be very supportive of me, hiring me for shows and flying me from Haiti to perform in Orlando, Jamaica, or wherever its latest performance was scheduled. Every penny I made was going to support our efforts, but although it was exhilarating, the work was sporadic and I still couldn't afford a car. So I continued to walk to and from work every day, making the trek down the hot and dusty road from the Caribbean Lodge to Grassroots United, where we still rented a small corner of space to carry out our programs. I often wondered on those walks how I could be better than the previous day. I would also stop at one of the street vendors I passed and pay twenty *gourdes,* about fifty cents back then, for a locally grown avocado. It was the most substantial and cheapest food I could find. It became my staple, though the monotony of my meals was a constant reminder of how thinly stretched my resources were.

Desperation sometimes led me to make choices I wouldn't have otherwise. One morning when I passed through Billy's makeshift kitchen, I noticed a lone tomato sitting next to a plastic bag. It had a huge bad spot on the side and I didn't think they would use it at the hotel, so I put it in my backpack and took it to work with me. That afternoon I enjoyed a half-rotten stolen tomato with my avocado, a meal that felt both indulgent and shameful. Deep down, I knew I had crossed a line. I might have told myself the hotel chef wasn't going to use it, but in my heart I still knew it was wrong. It took me years to admit to Billy what I had done.

He forgave me, and when he looks back, he shakes his head as he tells people stories of my determination. He says I inspired him and even reminded him of his mantra, "Always a little further." That phrase became a kind of rallying cry for both of us, a reminder to push past limits and keep striving. As our bond deepened, Billy became not just a supporter of my vision but an integral part of it. With his expertise in construction, he saw an opportunity to help expand our facilities and ensure our work had a stronger foundation. In 2012, his first big donation was of a piece of land he was renting, right next door to the hotel. We moved Deux Mains and the Elèv program there, occupying a few prefab containers with water damage that couldn't be used to build the hotel or the new burn center Billy was working on. Rather than let them go to waste, he donated them to us as well.

Our friends Andy and Emma from IDV offered to lead the construction of our new building project. With Billy's gift

Spring 2012. Second sandal workshop, Port-au-Prince, Haiti. I went from discussing the layout for the new space with Ian from EDV, to watching his team making the dream a reality as they built us our first real workshop with a stable roof. Weeks later we moved in, and I even got an outdoor office to share with the local cows.

we were going to transition from a lean-to facility with a completely worn-out tarp roof, into an actual building with a wood and tin roof. This new building was going to have a workshop for Deux Mains about ten times bigger than our original one, and the students would have an incredible tutoring facility to enjoy. The teams at IDV spent hundreds of hours building the workshop and tutoring center as well as an office, a warehouse for finished goods, and a little boutique where people could shop. The plot of land was huge. It had hundreds of moringa trees growing in the back, and we shared it with families of goats, sometimes a few pigs, and whatever other animals the herders could find. Billy's investment was a game changer for us. We were able to expand greatly, hiring more people and really focusing on our sandal production at Deux Mains.

The Caribbean Lodge became our shared world, where my future husband and I wove our lives together through endless projects and shared purpose. For three years we worked together on all sorts of projects, pouring our hearts into the work that connected us so deeply. But life had separate plans for us at that time, and eventually Billy's professional obligations called him back to the broader world. His business took him all over the globe, most often to Africa and the Middle East, while my roots were becoming firmly planted in Haiti. Deux Mains and REBUILD globally were flourishing, demanding my presence, while our growing partnerships in Florida required me to stay within easier reach of the States. We found ourselves caught between two worlds: his that spanned continents, and mine that had found its center in the heart of Haiti. So after years of working in unison, we transitioned to a long-distance relationship. One day before Billy left for a five-week trip, he called me outside and handed me a box filled with notecards.

"Whenever you feel sad or lonely, or forget how much I love you," he said, "open a card." Each card contained a poem, a song, a personal joke, or some other loving message. Billy's box of cards meant more than anything he ever could have bought me. They were his heart on paper, carefully written out for me to hold onto in his absence. I love all my cards, but one that especially touched me described how he saw me in the early days of Haiti, when I was at my worst, perpetually ill, covered in dirt, and drowning in work. He hadn't needed me to be polished and pristine, in a pretty dress with perfect makeup. Instead, he saw my heart and fell in love with my spirit and the dreams I carried for Haiti.

We loved each other from a distance over the next few years, as I poured all my energy into improving our business and focusing on our growth. As much as I wanted to be by Billy's side, my priority was to see our work in Haiti thrive, so I stayed put and began seeking new partnerships to move us forward.

The UN was still a powerful force in Port-au-Prince then, its presence both intimidating and alluring. By 2013, it was managing grants to smaller agencies it could partner with. One of its initiatives was a "livelihood project," focused on income generation for Haitian women. The money available in these programs was a lifeline for a small organizations like mine. But there was a catch: the competition for grants was fierce, and major players like the Red Cross and The World Food Program were in the mix. We were still a small, unknown organization, trying to carve out space in a sea of humanitarian giants. But we persevered and I refused to go unnoticed. I continued to attend the organized cluster meetings and loudly advocated for our small sandal workshop and its capacity to grow. After months and months of proposal writing and meetings, we got the news: Deux Mains was approved for a UN livelihood grant. Finally, we would receive substantial outside funding to pour into our operation.

With the extra cash from this business grant, I could now hire more craftswomen, expanding our team and empowering them to take on bigger challenges. But the real game changer was the opportunity to bring in experts, assistance I had been longing for. Until then, I had been teaching myself, piecing together what I could from the limited resources available. YouTube had become my best friend, offering tutorials and tips from sandal makers all over the world. But there was only so much a screen could teach me. I knew that what we were creating had the potential to be world-class, but we needed a deeper level of expertise to get there.

This opportunity from the UN gave me the chance to meet Ody, a Haitian sandal maker whose story was as incredible as his talent. Ody wasn't just an artisan. His gifts were so exceptional that the government of Haiti had sent him to Martinique for two years to learn the art of leatherwork when he was a young man, and upon returning to Haiti he had established himself as the key supplier of shoes, helmets, and bags for the UN. Now he had twenty years of experience. But in the aftermath of the earthquake, he had lost everything—his supplies, his workshop, and his home. The devastation was immense, but it didn't break his spirit.

When we met, we were both at a crossroads: I needed a trainer, someone who could guide us through the complexities of sandal making, and Ody needed a way to rebuild his life. It was clear from the start that we could offer each other exactly what the other needed. Ody had unmatched skill and was quick to understand the mission of our business; he wanted to help us succeed. He introduced the use of locally sourced Haitian leather and taught us the intricate art of sandal making with kindness, taking extra time to ensure everyone understood his instructions, especially those undertaking their first job. He didn't just teach; he reshaped our company. He dreamed up new sandal styles combining our tire soles with genuine leather, refined our processes, and helped us operate with greater professionalism. His contribution was more than just technical; with his zeal he became an integral and inspiring member of our team.

By the end of 2013 growth was everywhere, fragile but full of promise. Sandra and I had moved into our first apartment, in a neighborhood close to work. Ody was breathing new life into Deux Mains, and we were meeting lots of people interested in our work. However, I couldn't shake the feeling that the kids in our Elèv program deserved more support than Sandra and I could give. They were getting older, the program was getting bigger, and we couldn't continue to do both these projects alone any longer. That's when Emily came into our lives.

It didn't take me long to know that Emily was the kind of person we needed on the team. From the moment she stepped in, she dove straight into the heart of our work. I thought our programs were solid, but Emily's sharp eye quickly revealed cracks I hadn't noticed. She wasn't one to just sit behind a desk. Instead, she spent hours talking to teachers and sitting with the kids during tutoring sessions. She realized that, while we were helping, we could do more.

"Look," she said to me one afternoon, spreading her notes across the table. "We need to align our tutoring sessions with the school calendar and work more closely with our partner schools. The tutors need the lessons in advance so the kids can get the help they need *when* they need it." I nodded, feeling the aptness of her observation. We immediately began the process of revamping the program, ensuring that we were offering the after-school support students needed exactly when it mattered most. Emily's fresh perspective and dedication to the program helped it grow and thrive.

Emily's most impressive contribution wasn't overhauling the tutoring system—it was the way she invested in the people who made it all happen. She knew the key to success lay in empowering our Haitian team. So she focused on training our tutors, ensuring the lessons were targeted to the students' most pressing challenges. Rather than just filling gaps, her approach was to meet the kids where they were at, addressing their unique needs with precision. But she didn't stop there, she invested the time to make my ultimate dream come true. I wanted our charity to be fully Haitian-led, but I didn't have the connections in the academic world in Haiti to make it happen. Emily went to great lengths to travel around the city, meeting with great academic leaders and learning who might be interested in directing our program.

"I think I met the perfect person to take over Elèv," she said one day, her voice full of excitement. "Let's make your dream come true."

And with that, Djemson, a thoughtful and positive man with a deep love for education and an undeniable presence, became the Elèv Education Program Manager. He instantly earned the kids' respect and affection, and they adored him. He and Emily worked side by side, shaping a program that was not only comprehensive but deeply personal. Having a Haitian leader running our programs was, to me, the most relevant and sustainable way we could approach our work. Djemson didn't just lead with authority; he led with heart, understanding the nuances of his community in a way no outsider ever could. His leadership felt like the final piece of the puzzle, and the program flourished under his guidance.

With REBUILD globally thriving, I thought we needed to continue growing the team. Annie, a passionate young American woman working at Grassroots United, had originally come to Haiti in college, as part of an international internship program. While most students would have packed up and left after their project ended, Annie stayed. Haiti had gotten under her skin, and she was determined to do more to help. I asked around town if anyone knew much about her, and people spoke highly about her work as a program manager. She was known for her sharp mind, her knack for organizing, and her eye for fashion and jewelry design. She gladly accepted the new proposition I offered her and threw herself into the work. As a native of the Northeast, she was troubled that we made sandals only, a product that would be sold to a particular client, mainly in the summer. She was on a mission to expand what we sold and whom we could sell to. Of her many ideas for Deux Mains, her most brilliant contribution came from the least likely place, our trash bin. It was late one evening when Annie noticed it, a pile of discarded leather scraps shoved into the corner. She picked up a piece, turning it over in her hands.

"Why are we wasting this?" she asked, holding it up like she'd just discovered gold. That night she took the scraps home, and over the next few weeks she became obsessed. Every evening she'd sit on the floor of our small apartment, tracing and cutting, testing and failing. And then one day she got it. "Look at this," she said, her face glowing as she held up a pair of feather-shaped leather earrings. They were simple but stunning. She then motioned to a table behind her. Annie had designed an entirely new line of products. Earrings, bracelets, and a few small leather goods were scattered over the table. Suddenly, Deux Mains wasn't just about sandals anymore; we would have an accessory line as well.

The new products changed everything. We developed three teams: one for sandals, one for jewelry, and one for small leather goods. The workshop buzzed with activity, and our little company felt bigger than ever. Annie's idea didn't just save us from the seasonal slump; it opened a door we didn't even know existed. With every bracelet, every pouch, every earring crafted, we grew. We were no longer just a company; we were becoming a movement, a lifestyle brand that carried the spirit of Haiti in every product we made. The growth felt electric. And as the months turned into years, I realized we were inching closer to a destiny I'd always believed in: a factory and fashion brand in Haiti, bustling with opportunity, proving to the world that beauty and strength could rise from even the ashes the earthquake left behind.

CHAPTER 9

FAMILY AFFAIR

Family is family, whether it's the one you start out with,
the one you end up with, or the family you gain along the way.
Unknown

o

When my father was just five years old, he crossed the Atlantic Ocean, leaving behind the familiar hills of Italy for the promise of a new life in the United States. Accompanied by his parents and two older sisters, none of whom spoke English, he arrived on one of the last ships to dock at Ellis Island before it closed in 1954, a historic vessel named the *Christopher Columbus* that sailed from Naples to New York. Years later, my dad had not only become fluent in English, graduating from high school at the top of his class, but he became the first person in his family to go to college. His natural curiosity and work ethic drove him to excel, and he eventually became a research scientist at Lynell. In his time there he contributed to life-changing advancements, including surgical techniques that restore sight to those with cataracts. But my father was not one to stay within the lines of expectation.

After years of dedicated research, my father took a leap that surprised us all. Driven by his love for Italian cuisine and a yearning to reconnect with his heritage, he decided to leave the sterile labs of Lynell and embark on an entirely new journey. He moved our family to sunny South Florida, where he and my mom planned their first entrepreneurial venture, an Italian bakery and deli called Colombino's. From the very beginning, Colombino's was a family affair. My two sisters and I grew up learning the ropes of the business, taking orders, stocking shelves, and sometimes sneaking tastes of fresh cannoli cream when no one was looking. My parents insisted that we work alongside them, not just to help the business thrive but to teach us the value of hard work and pride in what we create.

My older sister Lori has always been the strong, polished, and determined one, the kind of person who commands attention the moment she walks into a room. She stayed close to home, living just down the street from the bakery after college, while I was off chasing adventures. After graduating from the University of Florida, she joined the police academy, and from day one she was a rising star. Quickly earning respect, she climbed the ranks from special-victims detective to police lieutenant at the West Palm Beach Police Department. In our twenties the contrast between us couldn't have been starker. While Lori patrolled the streets of West Palm, fighting crime and protecting the city, I was working as a bartender and go-go dancer. Lori would show up to family dinners in tailored suits and the latest fashion trends, while I rolled in wearing whatever sweatsuit I'd thrown on that morning.

She had the career and the plan, while I was still figuring out who I wanted to be.

I had been in Haiti several years when Lori came to visit me. I could tell she was nervous and out of her element. She clutched her seatbelt and glanced out the window at the dark, unfamiliar streets as we drove down the Airport Road that led to the Caribbean Lodge. Her world of order and structure didn't exactly mesh with the chaotic energy of Port-au-Prince. Theft was high in Haiti as desperation grew, and Billy had to take certain precautions at the hotel. The armed security guard standing at the entrance stopped Lori in her tracks. He held a shotgun, and while his uniform was well-worn, his expression was serious.

"Is this normal?" she asked, her voice low but tense.

"Completely," I said, shrugging. Lori frowned, eyeing the weapon.

"Does that thing even work?" I laughed and explained that since the earthquake, armed guards had become standard. Haiti's police force was stretched thin, and businesses relied on private security to keep things running smoothly. She didn't say much as we checked in, but I could tell the sight of that guard had unsettled her.

The next day Lori and I walked next door to Deux Mains and REBUILD. I'd been eager to show her what we had built, but I wasn't sure how she would react. As we walked into the space, the artisans paused their work to greet us with wide smiles and open arms, so excited to meet a member of my family from America. They pulled Lori into our circle, laughing and dancing as if they had known her for years. For the first time since she'd arrived, Lori relaxed. She watched me move around the workshop, checking on the team, laughing with them, and inspecting their work. She didn't say much, but I could see the wheels turning in her head.

"This is amazing," she finally said.

As Lori became more comfortable, she wandered around our space and her sharp eye for detail kicked in. She pointed to the boutique area, where sandals were stacked in mismatched containers, and shook her head.

"You're not showcasing these the way you should," she said. Before I could respond, she was pulling sandals out of their containers and rearranging them, transforming the space into a proper storefront. By the time she was finished, the boutique looked polished and inviting, a reflection of Lori's knack for organization and style.

My perfectly groomed sister was enticed by the sandals even more now. She told me about the women she worked with at the West Palm homeless shelter and how they could benefit from sandals like ours. Before her trip ended, Lori coordinated a donation of dozens of our Haitian-made sandals to the women in her community. Ensuring women at the homeless shelter would benefit from our work in Haiti brought us great pride. What neither of us knew at the time was that those same sandals would eventually find their way to the shelves of a high-end designer store in New York City. But as Lori stood in the workshop that day, surrounded by the passion and energy of my team, she didn't need to know the future. She was proud of what I had built, and I felt I had earned her respect.

My sisters and I have always had a bit of a competitive spirit with each other, and since Lori had come to Haiti, my younger sister Andrea made it her mission to visit me a few months later. It was the Christmas season, and I was so excited to have Andrea with me during this special time of the year. Her booming laugh would always fill a room, and her quick wit has made her the family comedian. Behind her humor, however, is a deeply sensitive soul, especially when it comes to animals. Andrea has channeled her love for them into Dream Believer Stables, an equestrian facility she built from the ground up. There she trains people to ride horses with confidence, care for these gentle giants, and "chase their dreams," as she loves to say. In addition to being excited about her visit, I wondered how her bold personality would adapt to Haiti's dusty streets, starving dogs, and raw realities, so different from the green pastures and sleek, well-fed horses she knew.

One morning as we drove down the main road, we passed a young girl, perhaps ten years old, collecting water from a community well. As the girl struggled to carry the heavy bucket, Andrea's laughter faded, and with a sweet naiveté she asked me what was going on. I tried to gently explain the dire poverty of Haiti.

"Most families here don't have access to running water and rely on wells for their daily needs," I said. Andrea didn't respond. She just stared out the window, uncharacteristically speechless, her eyes following the girl until she disappeared from view.

It was Christmas Eve and Deux Mains was closed. Andrea and I were just finishing up, tidying a few things in the now-quiet shop before heading back to the Caribbean Lodge. But then I heard a loud banging on the metal gate. I turned and saw Baka, a street kid I knew very well, his face pressed against the bars, eyes pleading.

"Let me in. I need to take a shower," he called out. I hesitated; I wanted to get Andrea back to the hotel before dark. But I know how much a shower means to a street kid, so I thought about opening for him. I jokingly picked up his arm and pretended to sniff his armpit.

I made a sour face and said, "Yup, you need a shower."

He laughed, his tough exterior cracking for a moment. I unlocked the gate and let him in. Baka followed me into our storage room, where I grabbed a clean t-shirt and handed it to him. A few minutes later, he emerged from his shower, with the same old clothes on and the new shirt rolled up in his pocket. Andrea, desperate to do something, gave him a granola bar she had in her bag, and he was off. Two days later, as we were on our way to a women's clinic, I saw Baka running toward us, a familiar figure on the busy streets. He had recognized the car Billy often let us borrow, and there he was, sprinting to catch up. He caught up, grabbed onto the open window, and held tightly.

With a proud grin on his face, he announced, "I sold my new shirt for fifty *gourdes*."

I couldn't help but mess with him a little. "You probably could have gotten a hundred for it," I teased. Andrea, sitting beside me, looked at us, confused. She didn't understand what we were saying, and not because we were speaking in Creole.

Later, as we drove on, she asked me, "Why aren't you mad that he sold the shirt you just gave him?" I thought about it for a moment before responding.

"Living in Haiti made me realize survival looks very different here. Baka probably needed food more than he needed a clean shirt that day. I can't get mad or try to dictate how he lives." I paused, looking out the window for a second, reflecting on the truth of those words. "I can't know what is best for street kids, so whenever I encounter them, I just try to show them as much respect and kindness as I can." Andrea sat quietly for a moment, taking it all in.

I would soon see that Andrea did not just learn; she also left her mark on us. Deux Mains was in the business of selling sandals, but we also started to make smaller sandals for children and donated them to the orphanages in the neighborhood because we knew a simple walk down the street could be a hazardous experience without some sort of protective footwear. However, the kids often ended up with sandals that were too big or too small, and I hated seeing our good intentions fall short. During one of our distributions at a local orphanage Andrea noticed our struggle. She pulled paper out of her backpack, had the kids stand on it, and began tracing their feet, creating a template we could use to make sandals that would fit each child. It was such a simple idea, but it changed everything. From then on, our donations made a real difference. Andrea may have come to Haiti as a visitor, but she left as someone who truly understood what it meant to care, to contribute, and to make an impact.

My sisters and I have a love for working and being part of something bigger. I think this stems from our childhood and the way our mom and dad invested in us. When we were young, we accompanied our parents to the bakery a few times a week. We had specific roles there; one of us would stand on a Pepsi crate so that we could reach the sink to wash the dishes, while another would sweep the floors. The lucky child would shadow my mom and use the cash register to check out customers. Our little deli was always alive with activity, full of fresh meats waiting to be sliced and Italian butter cookies waiting to be devoured. Waking up early on weekends and holidays, dragging ourselves into the deli while our friends were still asleep, didn't feel like a privilege at the time. But working in the bakery my parents built taught us all the rewarding values instilled by hard work and showed us firsthand the power of business.

Now that I've traveled the world and understand more about the access to work, I am even more grateful that I grew up in a country where people not only can find a job but, with a lot of focus and determination, start a business and teach their children the lessons of entrepreneurship. My father's parents understood this deeply, leaving Italy for this very reason. They were destitute, and no matter how hard they tried, opportunities for them in their own country were scarce. My grandparents arrived in the United States with nothing but their drive for a better life for themselves and their children. The details of their early days are mostly lost to time; my grandfather died before I was born, and I was young when my grandmother passed away. What I do know are fragments shared by my elders, glimpses into their struggles and triumphs as immigrants in a new land. If I could turn back time, I wouldn't have waited so long to ask questions and listen to stories about their lives. In those belated discoveries, I found an unexpected mirror in my grandmother: her spirit, I learned, blazed with the same fire that drives me.

Her name was Vincenza. She came from a small town, couldn't read or write in Italian, and never learned to speak English. Yet despite the odds against her, she still managed to work several jobs in upstate New York, where she and my grandfather ended up putting down roots. I couldn't believe that one of her jobs was in a factory, standing on an assembly line on a hard concrete floor, removing the pits from cherries at the Comstock Canning Factory. The assembly line never stopped. Cherries fell continually from a steel shaft, and Vincenza combed through them to find the pieces of pits that were missed, the final step in the operation before the fruit was processed and canned. Under her watch, no one ever opened a can of cherry pie filling and found a pit. She did this work for many years, earning $3.75 a day, sharing in her part of the American dream.

I think about my grandmother often. She arrived in a new country unable to speak the language, never attended school, and remained a member of the working poor her entire life. I try to imagine the sacrifices she made and the dreams she carried in her heart but never had the luxury to chase. I do know her struggles were not in vain. She was part of the working class of women who paved a path so deep and broad that just seventy years later, her granddaughter built and owns a factory in a foreign country. It makes me think about the parallels between her life and mine.

Like my grandmother, I've faced the daunting challenges of cultural differences, language barriers, and the ache of distance from home. Yet I've built a business in the fiercely competitive fashion industry, in a country where infrastructure barely exists. Comforts taken for granted in the developed world are nonexistent here, where many days we work without electricity and running water. Sometimes it feels as though we've been transported back to the 1800s, working without access to modern technology and dependable systems. Yet as I think of my grandmother, I draw strength from her story. If she could carve a life out of hardship and leave behind a legacy of possibility, then I too can endure, adapt, and persevere.

I especially needed to remind myself of her courage during the winter of 2013, when times were particularly difficult once again. The UN reported that nearly 400,000 people still lived in displacement camps, with fragile tents that were shredded to rags, and conditions remained deplorable. The cholera epidemic had raged through the city, killing more than 10,000 people, and it was still not done reigning its terror on Port-au Prince. Saturdays were our day to rest and step back from the daily chaos, but Ody was different. His love for the art form often brought him to the workshop on weekends to design new sandals and lose himself in a quiet world of creativity.

A nagging in my gut stirred me to go to Deux Mains early one November morning. Without hesitation Billy escorted me to the workshop. Even in the winter the sun beat forcefully on the path as we walked to the back of the shop. And then we saw him. Ody was lying on the floor, limp and delirious, in a pile of his own excrement. He had cholera, the silent killer that claims its victims within hours if left untreated. We had seen it before and knew its ruthlessness.

Billy moved first. "I'm calling Danny." When Danny arrived, Billy carefully lifted Ody as though he might shatter and placed him gently in the backseat of Danny's car. The silence on the drive to the cholera hospital was broken only by the sound of the tires on the uneven roads and Ody's faint, labored breaths.

Moments later we had arrived. The hospital was primitive, each bed covered by a plastic sheet with a hole in the middle so the patient could defecate right in bed. The smell was overwhelming, yet in spite of the conditions, patients had access to the right treatment here. The doctors and nurses worked relentlessly, their determination cutting through the hopelessness that hung in the air. Soon Ody was lying among the rows of patients, hooked up to IV bags, his face sunken, but he was alive. Days stretched into weeks, and slowly Ody began to recover. Visiting him when I could, I was grateful to watch the color return to his face and the strength seep back into his frame.

When he finally returned to us a month later, it was a small victory, but the fight was far from over. The city was simmering with frustration. The cholera epidemic only highlighted the intolerable conditions, and people took to the streets to protest, their cries echoing the desperation of a nation pushed to its limits. These were not just demonstrations. Barricading streets and burning tires were symbols of righteous resistance from a nation denied justice. It wasn't mayhem, though; it was a political strategy.

I later read in one of Haiti's most prominent magazines, *WOY*, that burning tires is the most aggressive form of nonviolent protest. "Tire burning is disruptive and creates dramatic images and serves as an expression of grievance, but it is contained. It's a political statement that no one can ignore." The journalist was right. The gesture was impossible to disregard. The more I learned about Haiti and its history,

Late 2013, outside our compound, Port-au-Prince, Haiti. Tires burning as a sign of protest against the deplorable conditions Haitians were being forced to live in.

the more I was beginning to understand the grievances of its people.

One sweltering summer day, the anticorruption demonstrations reached a crescendo and the streets of Port-au-Prince were completely impassable. Businesses locked their doors, children were ushered off the streets, and eventually even the airport ground to a halt. As a guest of this country, I have always made it my business not to judge or express my opinion about systems I didn't fully understand. Haiti's history, its political struggles, were far too complex for me to navigate with the ease of an insider. After living there for several years, however, I had not only heard about the corruption in Haitian courts and the lack of justice. I had also been a victim of them, forced to pay off certain members of the court who threatened violence and even jail time if I didn't comply with their demands for "payments." In Haiti, resistance wasn't a choice, it was survival. I stayed indoors during this time, but my activist heart was marching right alongside the people of Haiti.

The weight of Haiti's struggles was staggering, overwhelming even the bravest of hearts. But right at this time, in addition to witnessing the deep-rooted issues that were paralyzing the country, I was navigating a personal storm. My Uncle Joe had been killed in a tragic car accident, and this was the week of his funeral. I was desperate to mourn with my family and celebrate his life, but the demonstration had become so intense that the airport closed indefinitely and I was unable to fly home. I had never felt so trapped, so powerless.

My life had always been mobile, free. If I wanted to go somewhere, I went. But now, with no plane to board and no way out, I had to reckon with the raw reality of being stuck. For the first time, I felt what it was like to have my freedom curtailed, not by choice but by circumstance. It was a humbling education about what life is like without the rights and political freedoms I had always taken for granted. And yet, even as I told myself that these experiences would make me stronger, more empathetic, I felt myself unraveling. A numbness came over me and I started to shut down, withdrawing from any social interactions and losing all motivation. I didn't know how to contend with this situation.

Within a few days the protests began to calm down. Businesses reopened, streets were cleared of burning tires, and once again the runways at the Port-au-Prince airport were operational. With the return to normalcy my mom urged me to visit her mother, my Natna, in New York, even though I had missed the funeral.

"Your Natna would love the company," my mom said gently. She could hear the heaviness that lingered in my voice and added, "It'll do you good to be with family too." And so I went. My beloved Natna, a pioneer for women everywhere and now nearly one hundred years old, was as sharp as ever. I could sit with her for hours as she flipped through old photo albums recounting stories of a life richly lived. She had started her elementary education in a one-room schoolhouse, survived the Great Depression, and become the first female business office manager at St. Francis Hospital while raising the first of five children alone as my grandfather fought in the Second World War.

She wasn't just my grandmother; she was my best friend. Her stories were my refuge, her spirit my solace. The difficulties of the past weeks softened in her presence. My mom had been right, I needed this visit. Natna had lived through so much and emerged with grace; being close to her made me think I could find my way, too.

I would need to hold onto this reprieve, however, because another storm was brewing. Sandra was leaving Haiti. Sandra and I had shared years of living together at the Caribbean Lodge, we moved into our first apartment in Haiti together, and experienced more raw moments than I can recall. She walked right alongside me as we built strong and sustainable programs in Haiti, navigating the unpredictable tides of this beautiful yet complicated place with grace and determination. She wasn't just my employee; she was my anchor.

But Sandra had always been driven by her desire for education, and I knew all along she would someday head back to the United States to chase her dream of higher education. She had been accepted into the master's program she had worked to get into for years, and I had to plan for her departure. I had so many mixed emotions. Of course I was thrilled for her. I was inspired watching this woman I had grown to love like family take a bold step toward her future. But I couldn't ignore the knot tightening in my stomach. How was I going to manage without her? Sandra brought stability and conviction to everything we did. Replacing her felt impossible, but her departure wasn't something I could delay or avoid. I needed to prepare, for her sake and mine. I realized this transition wasn't just about Sandra leaving. It was about stepping back and looking towards the future of REBUILD globally and Deux Mains, even without her by my side.

CHAPTER 10

NEW BEGINNINGS

> Like slavery and apartheid, poverty is not natural.
> It is man-made and it can be overcome and
> eradicated by the actions of human beings.
> *Nelson Mandela*

○

The visit to New York had turned out to be more powerful than I could have imagined, both personally and professionally. Having the space to clear my head gave me the courage to face Sandra's departure head on and think about her replacement. My social circles in Haiti were still small, and as news of Sandra's move started circulating, people began talking. I had received many inquiries about her position, and one such email from a friend introduced me to Sarah, a young woman who lived in Haiti previously and might be interested in taking Sandra's position. Through that introduction, Sarah and I then became Facebook friends, chatting on Messenger every so often. I enjoyed getting to know her, and each time her name popped up in my messages, I'd throw myself on my bed and yell to Sandra, "Sarah messaged me!" It was ridiculous how excited I got, but there was something about her. Even through a screen, she radiated warmth and understanding. She *got* Haiti in a way that resonated deeply with me, and although I wasn't ready to face Sandra's leaving, I knew Sarah was someone special.

That summer I was with my Natna, Sarah was also in upstate New York helping with her family's business at the State Fair, as she had done every summer since she was a child. Realizing we would be in the state at the same time, we decided we had to meet in person. Being four hours away from each other, I found a meeting place halfway between us, borrowed my Natna's car, and headed to a little coffee shop in the middle of the state. I was excited to meet Sarah, but the drive was nerve-wracking as I pictured someone other than Sandra in this leadership position. I had one bad experience previously bringing someone new to Haiti, and it was something I was fearful of repeating. It distracted us from our mission and set us back. I was on edge about introducing anyone new into the company, especially in such a senior position. I arrived at the café first and was instantly annoyed that Sarah was late. Fifteen minutes later she burst through the door, her hair wild and her cheeks flushed. Breathless, she rushed over to my table with a lopsided smile.

"I'm so sorry! Traffic was insane!" she said loudly as she sat down. Something about her energy, chaotic but endearing, instantly put me at ease.

Within moments, the initial awkwardness of two strangers meeting melted away. This was intended to be a quick coffee meeting, but it turned into a marathon of stories, laughter, and ideas. Chatting like old friends, we quickly found a basis for mutual respect in our love of Haiti. As Sarah spoke, I could see two sides of her. There was small-town Sarah from upstate New York, who clearly adored her family and cherished her roots. And then there was Sarah with an insatiable curiosity about the world. She had initially learned French in high school, and in 2006 her mom begged her to join their church's annual mission to Haiti and serve as the group's translator. Grudgingly Sarah went, and to her surprise it was the beginning of a new life for her. She came home enthusiastic about international travel and decided to spend the next semester abroad in Senegal.

Sarah's eyes lit up as she described studying in a new culture, mastering French, and embracing a life far from anything familiar. "It wasn't just about learning the language," she said, "it was about the people, learning their humor and what they valued." It was an experience that eventually set her up for a life of living abroad. My admiration deepened as she spoke about her years traveling back and forth to Haiti; unlike me, she had been there before the 2010 earthquake and knew the country for something other than enduring a horrific natural disaster. She fell in love with the customs and the carefree Caribbean lifestyle, but it was the warmth of the people that drew her back time and time again. In 2008 she took a job working at the American University of the Caribbean in Les Cayes, a town in the south of Port-au-Prince, where she immersed herself in studying Creole and thus became proficient in her third language. Her passion for the country radiated from her, and I marveled at her dedication to learning new languages and understanding other cultures.

Sarah was living in Washington, D.C., when the earthquake struck. She felt a magnetic pull to return to the island, and a month later, she was back in Haiti. Serving as an interpreter for medical teams, she bridged the language gap between foreign doctors and Haitian patients in the hectic overflow clinics from General Hospital.

"It was intense," she admitted, "but I couldn't imagine being anywhere else." She eventually transitioned from a volunteer to an employee of the Methodist Church in Haiti. As she reminisced about the places she ate or visited, we realized how close we'd been during those years, sometimes just streets apart, though we'd never crossed paths until fate finally brought us together in that little coffee shop in New York. By the end of our conversation, I was truly impressed by her work ethic, her determination, and her dedication to learning. In addition to her accomplishments, though, I valued her heart.

When she finished sharing her stories with me, Sarah leaned forward, eager to learn more about our work. I explained the ins and outs of our business model, the way we used the best practices of the nonprofit sector and the business world to create change and invest in the long-term financial stability of families. She could tell our organization was something very different from anything else she had seen in Haiti. We weren't just a charity, or just a sandal brand, but something entirely new. I think the thing that moved her most was the collaborative way my team worked. She understood how important it was for me to have people who could get on board with our vision and culture.

"Everyone has a defined role and objective," I said, wrapping up the conversation, "but we always support each other, and we must share the same deep commitment to our vision."

Although I believed Sarah was an extraordinary individual, she could sense I was anxious about replacing Sandra. She paused before saying, "I can see how important this is to you. It sounds like what you've created is more than just jobs for people, it's a family." In that moment I knew she understood what I was trying to protect.

Sarah then suggested we try to spend a little more time together, so I could really get to know her before I made any final decisions.

"Unfortunately, I'm leaving tomorrow." I said, truly disappointed. "I need to spend a few days in Florida before going back to Haiti."

Sarah's face lit up. "I have friends in Florida!" she said. "Why don't I come with you? It'll give us more time together, and if you decide this isn't going to work out, I'll just go back to New York." At first I was taken aback by her suggestion, but then I realized it was a great idea, so I opened my computer and booked her a flight to the Sunshine State. As we finalized our plans, I couldn't help but feel that this trip would be a turning point.

The weeks in Orlando that followed were a whirlwind of connection and discovery. Sarah and I spent hours together, often deep in conversation over bottles of wine. I shared not only my grand vision for Deux Mains and RE-BUILD globally, but also the struggles that weighed me down. I was mostly worried about the business side of the operation and our ability to sustain all the challenges we had to endure. Haiti didn't offer the ideal conditions for a business to thrive, and the pressure was always on. Sarah listened without judgment, her insights sharp and without vague platitudes. She was the kind of person who would pour every ounce of herself into something she believed in. She admired my vision and the way a nonprofit and a business could work hand in hand to create change. I could tell she wanted to be part of it.

As I told her more about my budget, however, I sensed her hesitation. After graduate school she had begun to envision a very different path for herself. The State Department, perhaps, or some other polished role that reflected her degree and hard-earned expertise, with a salary that would match. The salary I offered was a fraction of what she could earn, and a 75 percent pay cut from her previous job in Haiti. With a new degree in hand and looming school debt, a low salary was daunting for her. Yet something about the vision, and maybe something about me, seemed to capture her. Sarah had that unmistakable look of someone on the brink of taking a leap of faith, and by the time our short stay in Florida had come to an end, we had packed our bags and headed for Haiti together.

I watched her during the plane ride, trying to gauge what was going through her mind. But instead of revealing her worries, she spent most of the flight cracking jokes and telling stories. She had me laughing so hard at one point that club soda shot out of my nose, leaving both of us doubled over in hysterics. When the wheels touched down in Port-au-Prince, the mood shifted. Sarah turned to me, her expression serious and resolute.

"I'll give you one year. After that, you'll have to make me a better offer." I couldn't help but smile. It wasn't just a promise; it was a challenge.

"Understood," I said and nodded. Deep down, I knew this was the beginning of a partnership that could change everything.

Minutes later, we were stepping off the plane, basking in the warmth of the Haitian sun, and breathing in the distinctive aroma that had become an intrinsic part of our lives. Deke, another member of the team, was there to greet us and take us home to Clercine, a neighborhood that held much history for our organization. Our apartment wasn't just a home; it was a hub of collaboration, a temporary house for volunteers, and a space where countless ideas had been born over shared meals and late-night talks. Sarah acclimated almost instantly. Getting out of our car, she took a deep breath and wandered down the street to the corner store, returning triumphantly a few minutes later with a couple of cold bottles of Prestige. We clinked them on the porch, the rhythmic sounds of the neighborhood providing the perfect backdrop as we toasted to a new beginning.

We set the empty bottles on the table and I led Sarah inside the house. Her first reaction was subtle but telling; there was a flicker of unease in her eyes. It wasn't exactly luxury living. Electricity was intermittent, flickering on for a few short hours each day, and the heat and mosquitoes were a constant annoyance. But I thought Sarah would see past all the inadequacies because I had given her a bedroom to herself. In anticipation for her arrival, we had dressed it up with modest improvements: a little improvised wooden nightstand, a mini battery-operated fan, and a standalone bed.

As she surveyed the bedroom I began to explain how Emily had played a huge role in making an significant improvement to this room. She moved into the house just as we were settling in. Back then, resources were even tighter, and we all slept on single mattresses on the floor. Emily had struggled with the setup from the beginning. After a few sleepless nights battling discomfort and crawling insects, she approached me with a heartfelt plea.

"Julie, could we please invest in bed frames?" Money was so scarce that even the smallest expenses felt hard to justify. And so, in what I thought was a creative compromise, I suggested we use concrete blocks to hoist up the beds. Emily's reaction was a mix of disbelief and laughter. Sandra laughed as well as they both declined the offer. A few weeks later, I realized I was asking too much of them and bought the bed frames. I could tell Sarah was processing all of this, her thoughtful eyes still scanning the modest room. If she had seen our sleeping arrangements before Emily intervened, I think she might have walked out on us. And yet she didn't say a word of complaint.

As I led Sarah into the kitchen, I felt a twinge of nervousness. It was functional, but far from what most people would expect. I walked her over to our deep freezer.

"Sarah," I said in a serious tone, "we utilize the few hours of power we have each day to freeze our groceries in here," I said, running my hand across its surface. "Then it acts as a refrigerator during the blackouts. Your groceries should stay cold long enough not to rot."

Sarah rolled her eyes and gave an audible sigh. She opened her mouth to speak, but at first nothing came out. "You're kidding, right?" she finally asked, half-laughing, half-hoping I'd say yes. Ignoring her question, I gestured to the wooden counter, where a single hot plate sat.

"That's our stove," I added with a sheepish smile. She couldn't believe we didn't have the means for an actual refrigerator or stove. She let out a soft laugh, but her shock was evident.

"I haven't seen one of these since undergrad!" she exclaimed.

She looked me straight in the eye and asked whether she could offer a few suggestions to make our living situation a little more bearable. I shrugged my shoulders.

"Sure," I said. "What do you have in mind?" Phone in hand, Sarah immediately started calling friends she had in Haiti, her voice confident as she asked about inverters and batteries. I couldn't help but be impressed. She hadn't even unpacked her bags yet, but here she was taking charge, finding solutions, and making life better. Sarah was going to be a force to be reckoned with, a partner who wasn't going to be afraid to roll up her sleeves and get to work.

The next morning, Sarah met the team at REBUILD globally and Deux Mains for the first time. As we walked through the high green gates that hid our oasis of creativity in the heart of Tabarre, I watched her face light up. She took in the expansive plot of land, our tutoring center to the right and the bustling workshop on the left. Despite the challenges of our location, Deux Mains stood as a beacon of possibility. The team greeted her warmly as she circled around the space speaking the language like a local, giving her an immediate personal connection to each person with whom she spoke. She wasn't an outsider here.

As Jolina and I gave her a tour of the workshop, office, tutoring center, and boutique, I noticed how naturally Sarah fit into the space. The artisans demonstrated their craft, sanding leather, threading straps, stitching sandals, and she watched with a mix of awe and respect. She asked thoughtful questions, and when Jolina recounted stories about the struggles and triumphs of the business, she listened intently.

Jolina then started to talk to Sarah about me as if I was no longer in the room. She told her about my eighteen-hour workdays, the weekends sacrificed, and the constant pressure I felt to keep the business open. She mentioned how I would sometime create fake orders just to keep the artisans busy, ensuring everyone had work even when there wasn't any. I had always assumed the team didn't know the lengths to which I went, but Jolina's words and Sarah's translation revealed the truth. They knew everything. With her language fluency, Sarah helped me see more deeply what the team felt. Jolina said the artisans believed it was my destiny to create jobs in Haiti.

"We got our lives back with this business," she told Sarah, her voice steady with conviction. When Sarah relayed Jolina's words to me, I saw my team through Sarah's lens, and I felt a profound sense of gratitude for the connection and respect that had quietly grown among us all. As we wrapped up the tour and headed back to the office, I smiled to myself. I knew I couldn't have asked for a better partner than Sarah to take the next steps with me. I handed her the blue bank bag that

 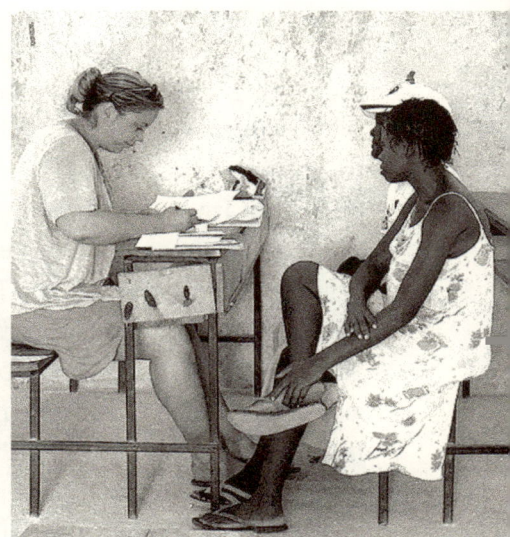

Spring 2014. Sarah getting right to work.

held all the petty cash, along with the keys to the shop, and jokingly said, "Don't mess it up."

I was entrusting Sarah with my life's work, and this was the biggest decision I had made in a long time. From the moment she stepped into our world, however, I could feel the winds of change. Within six months she had already left her mark. Her attention to detail, her understanding of the importance of producing great products, and her sensitivity to the situation of the artisans freed me up to focus on generating sales and bringing more income into the organizations. With the increase in revenue, I was able to provide Sarah with a small raise, as promised. It wasn't much, but it was a step forward. Even though we both hold graduate degrees, we worked for years below the poverty line, clinging to a shared belief that our business could change lives, not just for our team but for ourselves as well. She immersed herself completely. Her fluency in French and Creole broke down barriers, earning her immediate respect. She connected with people effortlessly, treating everyone she met with an equal measure of kindness and candor. That combination of humility and grit made her a force to be reckoned with.

CHAPTER 11

DEUX MAINS

○

By 2015, with the team functioning well and Sarah settling into her role beautifully, I decided to take a trip to visit some good friends in Colorado. While there, I found the inspiration for our business model in the most unexpected place, a brewery. Fat Tyre Beer Company was a thriving, employee-owned business in which every worker had a stake in the company. There was genuine pride on each face, from the bartenders to the tour guide, and the way they spoke about their work stayed with me. I couldn't shake the idea that this was the model we needed to pursue for Deux Mains.

But lawyer after lawyer told us we couldn't make that dream a reality in Haiti. They wanted me to retain 100% ownership of the business, as was the norm. But I refused to compromise. I believed with all my heart that an employee-owned model could transform lives. Our intention was not to create some foreign-run corporate business; rather it was to create a sense of ownership and possibility for those who dreamed of its inception. Sarah threw herself into the task, making call after call until she finally found a lawyer willing to listen. The plan to register and grow our business was ambitious, and the road ahead wasn't as smooth as we would have hoped.

Our sales depended heavily on the goodwill and curiosity of volunteers who visited our boutique in Haiti. These visits were typically orchestrated by organizations hosting mission teams visiting the country. Tara, a social butterfly working with short-term mission groups, managed a guest house close to our compound and wanted her mission teams to have unique experiences in Haiti, like visiting the Deux Mains workshop. She believed if they could see Haitian people working and thriving economically, it might rewrite the typical stories told on the mission field, and the story these visitors told themselves about the country.

Tara began bringing group after group to visit our workshop. The visits became more than just a tour and shopping experience; they were an immersion. Mission teams met the artisans, heard their stories, and witnessed resilience in action. For many, it was the first time they saw Haiti as a place not of need, but of possibility. Eventually Tara came to work with us, making tours of the Deux Mains workshop her focus. She had a way of connecting with visitors that was truly remarkable. She painted a picture of what we were building, a sustainable business that empowered women, changed lives, and gave hope. When groups walked into the workshop, however, the artisans took over. Their work spoke louder than anything Tara or any foreigner could have said. Watching the connection form between the visitors and our team was like watching seeds being planted. Perceptions were changing and sales were growing.

Within a year, the revenue generated from these tours allowed us to train and hire a dozen more women. Each new hire felt like a victory, and the women's pride and purpose was a daily reminder of the reason we started this journey. Claudette was one of our new hires. On her first day of work she arrived at the workshop with her head down, eyes glued to the floor and shoulders hunched over. She was wearing a pair of worn-out flat shoes, the toes frayed and riddled with holes. She listened attentively to the training and learned fast, but there was a sadness about her.

When payday came, however, Claudette changed. She walked into the workshop the following Monday with a newfound confidence, her lips painted bright pink and her feet adorned with shiny new shoes. The sadness that had once weighed her down seemed to have lifted, replaced by a spark of pride and joy. What moved me most, though, was watching her hand Jolina a bag full of candles, matches, and rice.

"For the orphanage," she said quietly. This was the first paycheck Claudette had ever earned, and not only did she provide for herself and her family, but she shared what little she had with others in need. Claudette's thoughtfulness and generosity, which came at great personal sacrifice, exemplified the kindness that made me fall in love with Haiti.

Foreigners who were able to see and experience this, assimilate into the culture and work alongside the people of Haiti were our most influential partners. Steph was one of the people who made a great impact on our work. She

June 2015, Deux Mains campus, Port-au-Prince, Haiti. With all the growth we were experiencing, we were able to open a new, one-of-a-kind boutique built completely from repurposed materials for customers in Haiti.

started a nonprofit organization, English in Mind, a unique language exchange program for teaching Creole to foreigners working in Haiti and English to Haitians eager to learn. They brought hundreds of volunteers to Haiti, and every visit included a stop at Deux Mains. These volunteers came to see what a healthy, growing business looked like in Port-au-Prince, and of course to shop our boutique. English in Mind had a network that stretched far and wide. On occasion it brought distinguished guests to our boutique. One guest was Heide, a New York City fashion model at the height of her career. She was stunning, not just in appearance but in spirit. Her rise to success could have been a movie script.

Heide had been scouted at a Britney Spears concert in her early teens and quickly became successful, regularly going to casting calls for high-fashion clients and gracing the cover of popular magazines. On her tour of the workshop, her admiration for the sandals was evident. She loved the artistry and the story behind the recycled-tire soles, a feature that always left visitors in awe. As she browsed the limited designs, however, she hesitated.

"These really are great," she said thoughtfully, "but I can't wear them to casting calls. They're just not fashion-forward enough." As a Florida native, she bought a pair to wear when she visited her family back home, but her words struck me. Until that moment, I had been so focused on making functional sandals that I hadn't considered their fashion appeal to a US market. Heide's comment wasn't just a critique; it highlighted an opportunity. Ody had made the sandals better in general with their leather uppers, while Annie had nudged us toward diversification, introducing jewelry and leather goods into our product line. With Heide's visit, an idea that had been quietly brewing solidified: we didn't have to be just a local sandal company anymore. We had the chance to become an international brand.

As it turned out, I wasn't the only one caught by a new idea. Heide returned to New York deeply moved by what she had seen in us. She fell in love with our mission, a stark contrast to the giveback model she was familiar with. She reflected on the cycle of dependency that traditional charity often perpetuated and saw, perhaps for the first time, the transformative power of sales. Every sandal sold meant more jobs, more independence, more freedom. Living in a city of eight million people, she realized the potential impact. If even a fraction of New Yorkers wore Deux Mains, the ripple effects in Haiti could be enormous. With her deep connections in the fashion world, Heide saw an opportunity to bridge the gap. She knew that if we could create designs that aligned with global fashion trends, she could help us break into the mainstream market.

A few days after her realization, she called. "You know, if you want something that's higher fashion than what you currently make, I would be willing to come back to Haiti and design a sandal for you." I couldn't believe her offer. Ideas spun in my mind about how we could expand and do more. But everyone on the team was so stretched already, and money was always so tight, that it seemed impossible for us to scale up by adding new designs. I explained my concerns to Heide, hesitating as I revealed how strapped for resources we were and how little support we might be able to offer her. But Heide wasn't deterred.

She booked a flight and returned to Haiti, and then she spent weeks helping us connect the dots in our story, the new sandal she was designing and all our other products. She introduced the trending concept of ethical fashion and showed us how we could be a part of the movement that was happening in the United States: "Imagine someone walking into a boutique in New York and falling in love with a design, not just for how it looks, but for the story it carries." Her vision was compelling. She painted a picture of a broader audience, people who valued fashion and purpose equally. Heide believed that by creating accessible, trend-forward designs, we could reach new markets, employ more Haitians, and amplify our impact.

As Heide helped me rethink the design side of Deux Mains, Sarah poured herself into building up the leadership team. I wanted her to help the team develop skills to prepare us for the demands of scaling up production. It soon became painfully obvious, however, that the Haitian management team were not the only ones who needed training and education. The earthquake that had devastated Haiti was years behind us, and our work had shifted from aiding disaster response to building a sustainable business, something I had not studied or prepared for. I watched other factories with celebrity backing and millions in investment fail under the weight of doing business in Haiti. I was determined that Deux Mains would not suffer the same fate. Yet as we grew, I felt increasingly out of my depth. Running a business, managing a charity, and navigating the complexities of international markets was a lot, and burnout was knocking on my door.

The people closest to me could see I needed help, and we all knew something had to change. Peter, an accomplished industrial engineer and venture capitalist who sat on the board of REBUILD globally, was also an entrepreneur-in-residence at the Crummer Graduate School of Business at Rollins College. He was deeply invested in our projects in Haiti and had a knack for seeing potential in people. He must have seen something in me because one day, after a REBUILD globally board meeting, he said, "You should go back to school. Get the tools you need to take Deux Mains to the next level." His words stayed with me, but the thought of adding school to all my responsibilities in Haiti felt overwhelming. Still, I took the plunge, and in the fall of 2017 I applied for and won the Martin Bell Scholarship for nonprofit leaders, a full scholarship to pursue an MBA from Rollins College. At the age of thirty-seven, I went back to class.

For nearly two years I lived a dual life, flying back and forth from a workshop in Haiti to a classroom in Orlando to complete my degree. My classes were like a mirror, reflecting the challenges we faced at Deux Mains while offering solutions I could implement in real time. The concepts I studied weren't abstract; they were tangible tools that directly influenced our work. Every time I returned to Haiti, I felt like I was bringing a valuable lesson back with me, a strategy, a new perspective, or a refined approach to leadership.

My MBA cohort was small, fewer than 20 members, but we weren't just a group of adult students; each of us brought a wealth of experience and personality, making us a tapestry of ideas, perspectives, and dreams. As I talked about the mission of Deux Mains and REBUILD globally, many of my classmates, moved by the purpose behind our work, offered their expertise or even got involved directly. Their encouragement fueled me during the toughest times. There were days when the weight of everything I was trying to do felt like too much, but then I'd find myself sitting in class, sharing stories from Haiti about Claudette's transformation, or Heide's bold vision for ethical fashion, and my classmates would light up. They understood the significance of our work and wanted to help carry it. In that room, surrounded by driven, compassionate people, I realized how interconnected our worlds could be.

Tadar, one classmate with a specialization in education, became a particularly influential person in our growing dreams for our work in Haiti. Our students were now older, and for the first time in our charity's history, these young men and women were preparing to graduate high school. They ranked at the top of their class, and they wanted to go to college or have access to good jobs. Once again, I found myself in uncharted territory. How could I help ten young people find their path in a country where opportunities were so scarce? Naturally, my first thought was that they could become artisans at the workshop, but these students had different dreams. With their education, they aspired to leadership roles and managerial positions. We needed a new plan.

Tadar listened intently as I laid out our new challenges. He studied each position at Deux Mains to see what opportunities we could offer graduating students that were more appropriate to their newly acquired degrees. He asked a lot of questions about our charity programs, our business, and the conditions in Haiti. After analyzing all the information, he offered a bold solution: enhance the curriculum and introduce activities that identify and nurture potential in our students. The eventual goal was a more personalized transition into the real world for the young people who graduate from our programs.

Tadar and Sarah worked with the leadership team at REBUILD globally to bring this vision to life. They revamped the curriculum and incorporated activities designed to sharpen critical thinking and creativity, introducing interactive modules focused on real-world problem solving. In that spirit, Sarah put together a STEM activity that required a lot of out-of-the-box thinking (STEM stands for science, technology, engineering, and mathematics). The challenge required students to construct weight-bearing bridges using only recycled materials and basic tools. To kick things off, she chose two team captains to lead the activity: Rony, always known for his natural charisma, and Lovely, another bright and promising student.

Rony's reaction was immediate and bold. He quickly selected his team, and under his breath he said, "Madame Sarah, just so you know, it's unfair to the other team that I am the captain, because any team I am on will win."

Sarah was surprised by his seemingly arrogant comment, since Rony didn't strike her as an egotist. She said, "Okay, we will see," and the activity began.

Rony took the game seriously, organized his team like a true leader, and won by a landslide. Sarah was secretly impressed, but because of his comment she was reluctant to show it. After the game, she walked into the office and told our HR manager how impressed she was with Rony's leadership skills. A few minutes later Rony walked into the office, and Sarah stopped talking.

Respectfully, Rony said, "As I told you, Madame Sarah, any team I am on will win."

Trying to maintain her composure, Sarah responded, "Rony, you really made me proud today, and you have so much potential, but one thing you can really work on is humility."

Rony looked back at her, a bit puzzled, and whispered, "I'm so sorry." Then he bowed his head, pressed his hands together, put them up to his chest in a gesture of respect, and in a solemn voice said, "Madam Sarah, any team I am on will win." Sarah barely managed to stifle her laughter. It was a light-hearted moment, but also a harbinger of things to come. Rony's confidence was not misplaced. Over the years he worked his way up the corporate ladder to become Sarah's protégé and eventually to hold the most senior position as the Operations Director of the Deux Mains factory.

The members of Rony's graduating class shared a love for Deux Mains and possessed a visionary DNA for excellence. Their deep love for the company, coupled with their notable academic skills, opened up brand-new opportunities for our young graduates who dreamed of becoming professionals. It may have started with simple games, but we were watching this passionate group prepare to step into adulthood and knew something transformative was needed to support their ambitions. A bridge between their after-school activities at REBUILD globally and their future careers had to be conceived so they could break free of the limitations imposed by Haiti's fragile economy.

With Tadar's assistance, the idea for the Deux Mains Academy was born. The program had clear objectives: support high school graduates as they pursued higher education, provide them with real-world work experience, and prepare them for leadership roles. We would achieve this in two phases. The first was to provide a paid three-month job training apprenticeship at Deux Mains. The students would learn all aspects of the company, and upon graduation from the program, they would enter phase two: a job at Deux Mains tailored to support their future careers. We achieved this by developing a work system that would act as a stepping stone for their dreams. The Deux Mains Academy graduates were offered flexible work hours to accommodate their college schedules and a program whereby Deux Mains matched each dollar they earned to help cover their college tuition. This way we could foster a sense of responsibility and empowerment in these young adults. With their jobs, they were able to contribute to their education financially and learn the value of hard work and a paycheck. Today this is more than just another program; it's a launching pad for the next generation of leaders who are driving change in Haiti. And at the heart of it all is Rony and his classmates, the visionaries who believed in their potential to change the world.

Lovely was one of the first students to walk through the doors of the new Deux Mains Academy, and from the very beginning it was clear she was special. Her journey with REBUILD globally began when the director at her school noticed her potential, a determination that couldn't be ignored. Lovely was unshakable, and her intelligence shone brightly. During her four years of schooling and tutoring at

REBUILD globally she approached each obstacle with calm confidence, and it wasn't long before she was excelling at everything that came her way. Whether it was mastering new skills, tackling complex problems, or showing up day after day, she was a standout.

Lovely quickly became a favorite among the management team at Deux Mains. As director of sales and boutique manager, Jolina was the first to have Lovely as her apprentice. As most of the apprentices did, Lovely worked part-time in the boutique learning about inventory, customer support, and merchandising, while continuing her education. Her dedication and ability to adapt made her excel under Jolina's leadership, but after a few weeks it was time for her to move on to other experiences.

Lovely had expressed an interest in being trained as an artisan, but Runel, our HR Manager, had other plans. He saw Lovely's leadership potential and knew she was management material. He was convinced she belonged in the office, helping shape the future of Deux Mains. Lovely, however, was hesitant, knowing Runel's tough management style. She feared she wouldn't measure up and that the pressure might be too much. But despite her doubts, she understood the opportunity she had. Being in the office, learning from Runel, and stepping into a role where she could expand her skills was something she couldn't pass up. She decided to give it a try.

The time she spent training in the office was a test of Lovely's resolve, but once again she exceeded all expectations. She outperformed on the challenges placed before her, mastering tasks, learning quickly, and stepping up whenever she was needed. Her work as the HR apprentice proved that she wasn't just capable; she was ready for more. When she graduated from the Deux Mains Academy, she was offered a job at Deux Mains working as the HR assistant. With a thirst for learning, she also continued her education at Université Américaine des Sciences Modernes d'Haïti (American University of Modern Sciences of Haiti) and balanced her budding career at Deux Mains. Over the next year, Runel trained her rigorously, instilling in her the skills and confidence needed for leadership. But just as Lovely was starting to find her footing, Runel left Haiti to pursue opportunities in Canada. The office, and the HR manager role, were now left vacant, and the responsibility that had once seemed so distant now sat squarely on Lovely's shoulders.

Sarah and the others on the management team saw this as a pivotal moment for Lovely. She was nearing graduation from university with her degree in Human Resource Management and had already proven herself to be diplomatic, and exceptionally capable. Sarah asked Lovely to consider applying for the job of HR manager. Lovely believed that seeing more Haitian women in leadership roles could make a difference in her country, but as a young woman in a society that often undervalues women in leadership roles, she didn't feel she could succeed in the position and openly shared those concerns with Sarah. Inspired by her honesty, Sarah sought additional support. She brought in one of Haiti's most well-respected female HR professionals to mentor Lovely one-on-one. This mentorship, combined with Sarah's unwavering belief in her, helped Lovely's confidence soar.

Port-au-Prince, Haiti. Lovely's graduation day from high school (2017) and university (2021).

One day Lovely approached Sarah with a heartfelt question: "Do you believe in me? I only want to hear that you think I am good at my job."

Sarah was slightly taken aback but responded without hesitation. "Lovely, I believe in you 100 percent." Those words ignited a fire in Lovely, who fully committed herself to the role. Now we knew it was inevitable that one day Lovely would lead the HR department at Deux Mains.

Today, she is the youngest woman to hold one of the highest positions on the management team. Her success not only underscores the impact of personalized training and mentorship but also serves as a blueprint for cultivating middle management talent from within. Lovely's journey inspired the introduction of specialist training opportunities at the Deux Mains Academy, proving that with the right support and belief, incredible leaders can emerge from graduates of our own charity programs.

The Deux Mains Academy emerged as a bold new chapter in our story. It was the promise of a career after graduation. In Haiti, where opportunities are scarce, this vision was not just ambitious; it was transformative. Each graduate was given direct access to a career at Deux Mains, but their paths were as diverse as their talents. Some became talented craftsmen and women, creating the unique products that defined the brand. Others stepped into roles that were crucial for building a thriving business as HR managers, executive assistants, materials and procurement managers, and trainers. The impact of the Academy has been profound. Today, more than half our employees have come from it. Those graduates who sought other professions have gone onto remarkable careers as lawyers, nurses, and hospitality managers. Their skills and experience, honed through years of meticulous training and real-world application, have made them highly sought after by businesses across the country. Our model of business development ensures we never lack talent or a management team at Deux Mains. This became the most magical part of our work in Haiti, and I would venture to say it is our greatest success.

CHAPTER 12

FASHION FORWARD

I always wondered why somebody didn't do something
about that; then I realized I was somebody.
Attributed to Lily Tomlin

○

Sarah never let the weight of her responsibilities in Haiti dull her devotion to the people she loved. One of her closest confidants, her mom Reenie, was no stranger to Haiti. Reenie's work in agricultural and educational projects in the country had begun long before Sarah ever set foot on the island. As a matter of fact, it was Reenie who orchestrated Sarah's first trip to Haiti all those years ago when she was just nineteen, so her French-fluent daughter could translate for her. But her trip in 2017 wasn't for work; it was just a visit to see her daughter.

On Reenie's second night in Haiti, we decided to set aside the relentless demands of life in Tabarre to unwind over wine and pizza at the home of Sarah's friend Lauren. Lauren lived in Pacot, a quaint neighborhood just outside the city center known for its charming, colonial-era gingerbread houses and cool mountain breezes. Sarah and Lauren's friendship dated back several years to their shared time working with the Methodist Church in Haiti. Lauren had an unforgettable blend of charisma and a Southern accent unique to the island. Her position at UMCOR, a big Methodist nonprofit organization, included accommodations that far surpassed our modest living situation. We were eager to get to her spacious, comfortable apartment.

Many organizations, including UMCOR, hired full-time drivers as standard practice to contend with the country's wild roads, an obstacle course filled with potholes, sharp turns, and general disarray. But at REBUILD and Deux Mains, such conveniences were beyond our modest budget. Instead, we relied on ourselves. After a few years and some driving lessons from Billy, I had gradually developed the confidence to tackle Haiti's daunting roadways. Sarah quickly followed suit, and her skills really flourished after we bought a Land Rover from a US embassy employee eager to offload his vehicle before being transferred to his next post. At such an affordable price it was a great exchange, or so I thought.

That evening Sarah jumped into the driver's seat and maneuvered us out of the congested streets of Tabarre and up the cobblestone paths that led to Pacot. When we arrived, we parked our Land Rover on the steep hill in front of Lauren's house and headed up the stairs, ready to relax. Sitting on Lauren's balcony overlooking the streets, with glasses of Dominican red wine in hand, we listened to our southern spitfire host talk about her day.

"Let me tell y'all something," she began, her country drawl dripping with exasperation. "My office had a fire drill today.

An *hour-long* fire drill. And after all that time and discussion, the big solution they came up with? 'Code Red.' That's it! 'Code. Red.'" She threw up her hands in mock disbelief, her frustration so vivid we couldn't help but laugh. As we chuckled, united over the absurdity of the outlandish protocol that accompanies working in Haiti, the universe threw us a curve ball.

A sharp, acrid smell cut through the night. Sarah was the first to notice.

"Lauren, what's that smell?" she asked, wrinkling her nose.

Lauren dismissed it with a wave. "Probably the neighbors burning trash," she said, and this was indeed a common occurrence in Haiti. But the smell grew stronger, harsher, unmistakably chemical. A ripple of unease passed among us. We knew something was wrong and ran to the balcony expecting to see a pile of burning trash, but we were aghast to see our Land Rover completely engulfed in flames. Lauren, quick-witted even in chaos, screamed in a joking but urgent tone, "CODE RED!" and we all bolted down the stairs, adrenaline propelling us.

Lauren grabbed a fire extinguisher from her apartment and we were able to douse the fire, but not before it had consumed the vehicle, leaving nothing but charred metal and melted plastic. We learned later that a spark beneath the dashboard had ignited the blaze, and with the seat pushed forward against the steering wheel, the upholstery had quickly caught fire. Without the Land Rover we had lost our freedom, our safety, and a vital tool for work.

The next day, a group of good friends from Grassroots United came to help us recover our car. They arrived at the scene, where the Land Rover was melted to the pavement, and they towed it back to our workshop, where it remained untouched for years.

Even though our charity found its rhythm, with donations steady and generous and the sales of sandals and jewelry keeping the wheels of our business turning, the car fire made me realize our infrastructure was fragile, too fragile to support our growing mission. In just one evening, we had lost something vital to our survival and we couldn't afford to replace it. The sting of our vulnerability stayed with me. It was a wakeup call that our business couldn't rely solely on profits from product sales. If we wanted a safe and sustainable future, I needed substantial funding. I needed operating capital. The next challenge was finding it. Who in Haiti had the resources and was investing in business development and job creation all these years after the earthquake, and more importantly, how could we connect with them?

It was 2017 and people were out most nights, making connections more naturally at the bars and restaurants than in boardrooms. Spending our nights out in the city led to new friendships with people working with the large organizations, and through them we learned USAID was still investing heavily in Haiti. More surprisingly, we learned the foreign aid agency had been watching us from afar. What we were accomplishing was extraordinary: a foreign woman who came as a disaster responder but stayed to build a business in Haiti was rare. This kind of perseverance didn't go unnoticed.

However, turning USAID's interest into a partnership wasn't easy. The process was long and grueling, yet persistence paid off. After a few dozen meetings, USAID decided that Deux Mains did have the capacity to grow and would be a worthwhile investment in Haiti. This was the catalyst for things to change dramatically for us. The first contribution USAID made was in the form of Heinz, a manufacturing specialist whom they sent to Haiti to conduct an initial audit of our workshop. Heinz was a German who had spent years building factories in Africa. He was crass and hard to work with, but he was talented and knew his job well. The first time he stepped into our workshop, he barely looked around before declaring, "This space is too small. You can't even handle your current orders, let alone grow." He wasn't wrong. Then came his next critique: "If you want to become a legitimate factory, you need better equipment and a bigger space. Otherwise, this vision of yours won't work."

As ruthless as his words and temperament were, they were the motivation I needed to find a new place and build an actual factory. I gave Sarah the task of finding us another location and she began the hunt for the new building. Factory spaces in our price range weren't easy to come by, and the process was slow. I was impatient and nervous that if we didn't move quickly enough, USAID would pull its investment. My frustration motivated Sarah to hire a realtor to help us search for a factory space that met our requirements and was ready for us to move to immediately. The realtor introduced us to Patrick, a man who owned several commercial properties in the area that had miraculously survived the earthquake.

"One of my complexes has a few possible properties," he said, "and one of them might be exactly what you are looking for." The only catch was that it was very close to Cité Soleil, the poorest slum in all of Haiti, known for its violence and gang activity.

The proximity gave us pause, but Patrick assured us the situation was changing. The business leaders in the area had petitioned for a police station, and their efforts had been rewarded. In fact, the new police station was next to the compound Patrick was thinking would be right for Deux Mains. The local business owners had also commissioned a school for children in Cité Soleil, including the children of gang leaders, which, too, was close to this factory compound. The school gave us an unexpected layer of protection. With their children attending, the gangs had an unspoken reason to keep the peace.

Patrick led us through a series of buildings, his excitement genuine as we told him stories about the sandals and leather goods we made and our dreams of growth. There was an ease about him, a calm certainty that made me believe we could trust him instantly, and I could tell he was impressed with our business.

Patrick hesitated before taking us to the second floor of an unfinished building that needed a lot of renovations. This was the last building he had to show us, and it was also the biggest, a former World Food Program warehouse.

"I'm not sure you'll want this one," he admitted. "Most people won't touch a second floor after the earthquake." His words hung in the air. The earthquake of 2010 had left scars not just in the earth but in the hearts of the people. Many Haitians refused to set foot in upper stories of buildings, their memories too vivid, their fears too real. But as we stood there, surrounded by cobwebs and dust dancing in the sunlight, I saw something else. This was more than an old warehouse. It was possibility. I could already hear the hum of sewing machines and see our team cutting leather and stitching sandals. I came back down to reality surveying the space. It was big. So big, in fact, that I didn't think there would be any way we could afford it.

I hesitated before asking, "How much?" Patrick pulled out his calculator, his fingers pressing keys as he worked through the numbers. Finally, he looked up and gave us the total. I stared at him, stunned. It was affordable. Without thinking I grabbed Sarah's hand and exclaimed, "We'll take it!" But catching myself, I blurted out, "Why is it so cheap?"

Patrick smiled, his eyes serious but kind. "Because this is what Haiti needs," he said simply.

As a man of great importance in the development of his country, Patrick spoke with authority and his words touched me deeply. A few days later, the entire team gathered as I unlocked the door to our future home. The anticipation was electric, no fear of the second floor, but a feeling of our bright future to come. Some of the younger team members ran alongside the wall, jumping and hitting the rafters with their hands, laughter filling the space. Others just stared in disbelief, taking it all in. And then, as if by some unspoken agreement, we found ourselves standing in a circle in the middle of the room holding hands and singing "Ala ou Gran" ("How Great Thou Art") Our voices echoed through the emptiness of the building.

As amazing as this development was for us, securing a new space was just the first step of the transition we needed to make to become a sustainable functional factory, according to Heinz. We needed machines, and lots of them. Their cost alone would be significant, but the sort of changes he envisioned for us to produce at competitive speed and with real factory precision would also be costly. Heinz knew our prices and products would need to compete with those of other manufacturers if we were to be successful, and we needed more cash than just the investment from USAID. Luckily, USAID's investment did accrue to more than just Heinz and financial support; it gave us the credibility to find outside capital, which we now needed to make all this happen. Doors that had once been closed began to open, and other financial backers grew interested in investing in our business.

Soon after we moved into our new building, I received an unexpected invitation from the Clinton Global Initiative to participate in a pitch competition for women-owned Haitian businesses. The opportunity held enormous potential. After weeks of preparation, I stood in front of a group of investors in New York City, confidently pitching our plans for job creation and business growth in Haiti. After each other business owner had offered their dreams for their company in turn, we all waited with anticipation for the judges to evaluate our plans and give the outcome. When "Deux Mains!" was called out, I fell to my knees, humbled to be standing next to other businesswomen from Haiti. We won $30,000 to invest in our new factory. With two investors on our docket, our momentum was being solidified.

Soon after that we once again caught the attention of the United Nations. Inspired by our vision of growth, the UN reached out with an investment of its own. As the year drew to a close, my courage also grew. We still needed hundreds of thousands of dollars to build the factory the way we dreamed. I scoured the internet, looking for any opportunity to match the initial USAID funding. In my research, I found a business grant program established by one of my heroes in the ethical fashion movement, Eileen Fisher. To support women in business who wanted to create positive social and environmental change, Fisher had established the Eileen Fisher Women-Owned Business grant. I knew this would be a perfect application for me to submit, and after a few weeks of waiting to hear back, once again we found ourselves the winners of a prestigious award. Another step forward, another validation that what we were building mattered. These investments were the foundation that allowed us to scale up our company and build our new factory.

More powerful than just the influx of capital that propelled us forward, however, were the people. Talent from all over the world converged in Haiti, bringing fresh perspective and skills. Among them was Lore, a schoolteacher from Belgium whose journey into our Deux Mains family was as unexpected as it was profound for us. With a wanderer's heart, Lore wanted to do a little exploring before she settled down. When an uncle who was working for a water charity in Haiti asked her to visit during her summer break, she jumped at the chance. Before she knew it, she was on a plane to Haiti, ready to embrace the unknown.

A native Flemish speaker, Lore easily adapted to the Creole language and quickly became comfortable enough to volunteer in a local school. She poured all her heart and experience into the classroom that summer, and the Caribbean Island equally captivated her. She soon realized it wasn't just the vibrant Haitian culture or the work that was stealing her affection; it was Venel, a kindhearted mechanic whose resilience shone through his quiet demeanor.

Venel, like many others, had suffered immeasurable loss during the earthquake, including the death of his wife. But for the sake of his son Kiki, he was determined to recover and rebuild his life. Lore and Venel had an immediate and undeniable connection, yet she had responsibilities back in Belgium and needed to return for her teaching job. The two made a plan to speak daily on Skype and WhatsApp, and for the next three years they sustained a long-distance relationship, able to see each other only in the summer and on school holidays.

When Lore was unable to bear the separation any longer, she quit her teaching job in Belgium and moved to Haiti to marry Venel. The newlyweds decided to relocate to Port-au-Prince to be closer to Venel's family and a good school for Kiki. The Nazon neighborhood, near downtown, was a stark contrast to the countryside, but Lore was determined to assimilate by attending community events and finding her place in the heart of the city. A few months after her move to Nazon, she attended a local artisan fair, stumbled upon the Deux Mains booth, and met Sarah. The handcrafted sandals immediately caught her eye, but it was the history behind the brand that left her deeply inspired. With her experience in Haiti and her understanding of the deep need for jobs, Lore was enthralled with our story.

Lore's trip to the artisan fair also awakened an interest she hadn't pursued in years, fashion and handbag design. She couldn't stop wondering whether there might be a place for her at Deux Mains. A few weeks later, Lore visited the Deux Mains workshop, ostensibly to buy sandals for Kiki, but really to satisfy her curiosity about the company that only grew. Sarah welcomed her warmly, giving her a tour of the space, telling her all about the upcoming week when I was coming to Haiti with a team of models, professional hair and makeup artists, and a photography team for a photoshoot. We were unveiling a new Deux Mains collection, and excitement was building. However, there was one problem: the prototypes for our new leather handbags weren't ready.

Sensing an opportunity, Lore nervously offered her help, and the team gratefully accepted. Lore demonstrated the sewing techniques and design ideas she'd once mastered, and to her surprise, the team embraced her suggestions with enthusiasm. The next day I hired her. Her natural talent and collaborative spirit made her an instant asset. Over the following years, she worked closely with Daphnee and Michel, our sample maker and handbag team lead. Together, they designed stunning leather handbags and accessories, breathing new life into Deux Mains' product lines. With every stitch made, Lore became a part of the legacy we were building, one that used fashion as a force for good, a weapon against poverty, and a symbol of hope for Haiti.

The time had arrived for us to become the company we were intended to be. We didn't just want to be a business that celebrated the tenacity of earthquake survivors. We dreamed of more, of being a global brand that would showcase the ancestral wisdom and artistry of Haitian craftspeople. We wanted to be a symbol of innovation, contributing not only to the survival of individuals, but to the idea of economic development in Haiti itself.

Each business decision was predicated on that vision. The products we made had to be as authentic as the two hands that crafted them. Each sandal sole cut from upcycled tires had to carry its own unique story of rolling through the streets of Port-au-Prince. The leather we molded by hand had to be responsibly sourced and of the highest quality. When it came to our handbag collection, we had to draw inspiration from Haiti's ancient traditions, designing accessories that were both strong and elegant. Every detail mattered. Every decision had a ripple effect, influencing the livelihoods of many people.

With all of Lore's contributions to the team, Sarah was able to take on more of my responsibilities, so I made the bittersweet decision to move back to the US in order to concentrate on growing our customer base and getting more investment to fuel our expansion. Life back in the States was strange and scary. It felt more foreign than Haiti, which had become my home. I had grown accustomed to my life there, and I had found purpose, each day filled with challenges that felt deeply meaningful. Now I was unsure how to assimilate. I no longer had a home, or the means to establish an office stateside for Deux Mains and REBUILD globally. Billy was still working thousands of miles away, and I struggled to find my footing in a community that didn't share my experiences or understand the weight of what I'd been through.

But amid the discord I was facing in this transition, I found hope. My alma mater Rollins College was promoting a social entrepreneurship program to which I could profoundly relate. It valued businesses like Deux Mains, and it was taking a leadership role in educating students about the importance of these sorts of companies. I reached out to my old professor, letting her know I was back in Orlando, and soon I found myself back in familiar classrooms, not as a student but as a speaker, sharing real-world insights with bright-eyed undergraduates. Before long, I was judging pitch competitions in which students presented their own world-changing ideas, seeing in their faces the same passion that had driven me to Haiti.

The real game changer was our ability to offer internships to Rollins students. For me, it was like finding reinforcements when I needed them most, eager young minds ready to pour their energy into our mission. For the students, it was a chance to step beyond theory and into the messy, inspiring work of social change. But coordinating it all presented its own challenges. Without an office or team in the States, I was running this growing network from my laptop, often working from coffee shops or a friend's kitchen table. Once again, however, my church came to the rescue. Two small storage offices were tucked away next to the community room, growing dusty, and within days church members had cleared them out and handed me the keys, no rent, no strings attached.

Finally, we had a real home base in the United States, a place where interns could gather, where we could host meetings, where I could spread out our work without taking over someone's dining room table. Best of all, every dollar we saved on rent was another dollar we could send to Haiti, where it was needed most. With the talent pipeline of interns coming from Rollins, our new office foundation was being firmly set.

My first intern, Thais, was pursuing environmental studies and sustainable urbanism. She was as committed to our mission as I was, despite the internship's not being salaried. While I deeply appreciated her dedication, it troubled me that I could offer only unpaid internships. That model, although common at the time, clashed with the very values that Deux Mains and REBUILD globally stood for. Determined to change this, I applied for a business grant and was able to secure enough funding to build a US staff. Eventually, I was able to hire Thais as our brand merchandising manager. Her patience and belief in our work were humbling. Paid or unpaid, she worked diligently to share our vision and our products with communities across Florida and the East Coast, becoming an integral member of our team.

Soon I was flying in and out of Haiti so often that my loyalties were torn between the needs of the US office and those of our growing factory. I wanted to help ensure we were building a healthy and sustainable factory in Haiti, yet I knew the survival of our business depended on something far less tangible, my ability to be a great saleswoman. Thais became a critical bridge, anchoring our efforts in Orlando. With her understanding of sustainable fashion, she helped embed the local Florida community into the heartbeat of Deux Mains. She connected with clients, arranged pop-up stores, and sold to bigger stores that could carry our brand.

One of her early victories was selling our sandals at Ron Jon Surf Shop in Cocoa Beach. Even though we didn't have any name recognition as a brand, we didn't let that hold us back. We were excited for Ron Jon's customers to be a part of this mission. We proudly marketed the impact, highlighting how each pair of sandals kept rubber out of landfills and waterways, protecting fragile ecosystems and reducing pollution. The sandals were a symbol, proof that creativity could give waste a useful second life. And Ron Jon was proof that established brands could offer incredible partnerships for us.

Ron Jon gave us the first opportunity to tell our story in a widely recognized retail outlet, and it lit a fire in those of us working on the US side of the operation. Up in New York, Heide was still determined to catapult Deux Mains into the city's spotlight. She was leveraging her contacts and reputation to organize the first-ever sustainable-fashion event at Madison Square Garden. It was a gathering of some of the biggest names in the industry, and with this sort of exposure, I was starting to believe that Deux Mains could be a powerful voice for the ethical fashion movement.

Meanwhile, back in Orlando, our efforts were also gaining momentum. I was invited to speak at many social entrepreneurship events, sharing not just the mission of Deux Mains and REBUILD globally, but the belief that sustainable business and nontraditional charity could rewrite narratives. Haiti wasn't just a country in need of aid, but a place of untapped potential and entrepreneurial spirit.

At Rollins College the following year, I walked into a buzzing MBA classroom where a group of students were presenting their final consulting project for Deux Mains. It was a proud moment, seeing my company on the big screen and hearing students discuss the future of what we were building. I knew Deux Mains was a unique choice—it had been the only business on the list of options that could truly be considered a social enterprise. Most of the other companies from which students could choose were massive corporations with towering profits, but Deux Mains was different.

What stood out to me most was the enthusiasm of one particular woman in the group, Isabel. She was determined that Deux Mains should be the project they chose. While others may have been drawn to the glitz of large corporations, Isabel saw the heart of what we were doing, and it was her push that led her group to choose us. She dove right into her insights about the company and I was captivated. She offered fresh perspectives I hadn't considered, and I knew immediately that I wanted her on my team. After analyzing my company, the students certainly gave me a lot to think about, but as impressed as I was, I couldn't ignore what was missing. When it was my turn to speak, I posed a simple question.

"Have any of you worn a pair of our sandals, carried our handbags, or even seen our products in person?" Isabel's face flushed with realization. It was such an obvious oversight, and yet no one in the group ever considered immersing themselves in the products before consulting on the company.

Isabel later confessed it was a lesson she would never forget. Working to make change in a company requires hands-on experience, and the team had missed that. The interaction was powerful for both of us.

A few months later, I offered Isabel a position at our company, and she accepted a role as our first-ever social media manager. With her natural talent, she rapidly grew into a communications powerhouse, bringing a strategic brilliance that our US team soon began to rely on. Isabel's first mission was to bring clarity to our story. Sitting in a small corner of our church office for hours, surrounded by sticky notes and whiteboards, Isabel mapped out the threads of our tale.

"We're trying to tell people everything at once," she explained one afternoon, gesturing to the jumble of notes before her. "About REBUILD globally's education programs, Deux Mains' production, the environmental impact, the employment creation—it's all important, but it's too much for someone to grasp in one moment." She wanted to make sure people could digest what we were trying to say and understand why we needed both a charity and a business to get the results we were able to achieve.

Ready to approach our messaging challenges head on, she knew she had to start with me. With characteristic gentleness, she held a mirror up to my own self-imposed perfectionism.

"Julie," she said, spreading out our latest impact reports, "you're trying to solve every problem at once. The most eco-friendly materials, the most jobs possible, the broadest community impact... it's just too much for even our nimble agency to handle." Her words hit home, especially when she reminded me of something that had stuck with me for years, the words of the Haitian woman who had told me plainly, "I don't need water, I need a job." Isabel's insight helped me see that while our commitment to ethical practices was crucial, trying to be everything to everyone could be the enemy of progress. I needed to temper and focus my energy.

Next, she focused on describing our mission not as two separate entities, a charity and a business, but as complementary forces working together toward the same goal: to build a responsible and dignified pathway out of poverty. To immerse herself in the mission, Isabel traveled to Haiti herself. Watching the tutoring sessions, hearing the stories of resilience, and witnessing firsthand the impact of dignified employment solidified her commitment to the work. Our classroom conversation now came full circle: Isabel didn't just talk about Deux Mains and REBUILD globally; she lived it. Her drive pushed her to new heights. She chose the parts of our story to elevate and figured out how to help people see the difference between our charitable initiatives and our business. She also insisted on finding every opportunity for me to amplify our mission. This led her to discover an opportunity for me to give a TEDx Talk at Florida International University (FIU), my undergraduate alma mater. Though public speaking on such a grand stage terrified me, Isabel was relentless in her encouragement.

Thanks to her persistence, I stepped onto that stage and described the journey of REBUILD globally and Deux Mains to the audience. Having the US team's participation in our work reminded me that while our path was often uncertain, the people who believed in us, both in Haiti and in the United States, are the ones keeping the dream alive.

CHAPTER 13

FAITH OR FASHION?

May God bless us with enough foolishness to believe that we can make a difference in the world—so that we can do what others claim cannot be done, to bring justice and kindness to all. Amen.
Franciscan Benediction

o

Back in Haiti we found ourselves at a unique intersection. Our boutique wasn't frequented by the typical Ron Jon patron or someone walking through the streets of New York City curious about an emerging new storefront. We were not trying to build bridges between those who follow fashion's changing tides; rather, we catered to missionaries. Our customers traveled oceans away from the trending epicenters of everyday life hoping to bring some sort of love and faith to island neighbors they had yet to meet. The missionary customers who wandered into our space were often new to the concept that our business was a form of ministry, a way to fulfill that ache to connect to faith, but after seeing how Deux Mains supported families, many viewed it as a tangible way to work in Haiti.

Some others, however, found it hard to imagine that I could find solace in focusing on a craft that tethered me to the beauty of the island and its people but didn't include reading bible verses. But designing bags and sandals that had a profound financial impact on someone's life was the way to fulfil a purpose I felt drawn to. It also gave me comfort to know people who used Deux Mains bags or strolled along in our tire-soled sandals carried a piece of our dream with them. Their purchases became my strength, reminding me I was there to help tell stories from Haiti, not just through words but through the artistry we poured into each design. Every creation was a statement, not necessarily of faith, but of intention. And in that intention, I found a renewed connection to God, to my work, and to the greater purpose of our business.

Using fashion to approach my life and work was such a different experience for me. Before I started Deux Mains, I had given little thought to my fashion choices. As a professional dancer, I had tailored my world around movement, not style. My wardrobe was the unofficial uniform of dancers everywhere—oversized t-shirts, often with the neck cut open, and comfortable sweatpants. Beyond the dance studio, my style ethos was equally unremarkable: be comfortable first, blend in second. Back then, I couldn't imagine that anything I wore would make a statement about what I believed. But Haiti has a way of teaching me lessons I didn't know I needed. And as the truth dawned that financial freedom brought so much richness to life, my perspective shifted, showing me that fashion could be far more than vanity; it could be a key to economic freedom, which became inseparable from my spiritual purpose.

Though many missionaries embraced this vision, I still encountered sincere questions about our approach: "How does your business serve God in Haiti?" or "How does your business advance the Kingdom?" These types of queries opened the doors to difficult conversations, and they were a scary reminder of similar challenges I'd faced in 2010 when my methods were different from those of the traditional disaster responders. I was crushed that I was at another crossroads, where my philosophies of working in Haiti were doubted by those around me. Was our form of Christianity so different that it wasn't good enough for some Christians in our sector?

Even though I was committed to our model of development and the work to which I felt drawn in Haiti, being questioned even occasionally about the validity of that work was painful, and I became terrified of losing missionary customers. By this time our artisan team had grown dramatically, and I couldn't afford not to grow our customer base, let alone lose any of it. I became desperate for a new sort of customer who might appreciate our products and mission without requiring us to fit into a particular mold of ministry. But with no background in the real fashion world, the best thing I could do was lean on the connections I was making. I began to pay closer attention to the people in the fashion industry who had successfully reached broader markets and who had an interest in Haiti.

Then an extraordinary opportunity came our way: the arrival of the internationally famed fashion designer and activist Kenneth Cole. I have always admired Cole for his bold stance on social issues and couldn't believe he was working in Haiti. He had arranged a trip, accompanied by a few members of his team, to visit a hospital he had been supporting for years. He also planned to invest in the business scene in Haiti by opening a new Kenneth Cole store in an affluent area of Pétion-Ville.

His first evening back in Haiti, Cole learned there was a leather-working factory close to the hotel where he was staying. Something about the story, our handcrafted work, our determination to uplift the community with jobs in the fashion sector, caught his attention. By morning his curiosity had turned to action, and his team arranged a visit to our workshop. I remember clearly the moment Kenneth Cole walked through our doors. It was surreal for us, but there he was, standing in the doorway of our workshop that was stocked with hand tools and had the faint smell of leather in the air. Cole was approachable, taking the time to listen as the team walked him through our process. He watched intently as they demonstrated our hand-crafted techniques. He nodded and smiled, occasionally offering bits of advice along the way. He wasn't just a spectator; he was absorbing, imagining, and creating alongside them.

After the tour, he sat down on our faded wooden workbench next to Jesselie, an original craftswoman on the Deux Mains team, and gestured for a piece of pattern paper. Sarah scrambled, only to realize we didn't have any. Improvising, she handed him a piece of computer paper. Without hesitation Cole grabbed a pencil and began sketching a sandal. His hands moved with precision, and minutes later he held up the finished drawing. Smiling, he said, "I want Deux Mains to produce this sandal for me." Everyone in the room held their breath.

He explained that this design would be sold in his new store in Haiti, emphasizing how critical it was to him that this store support the local economy and local artistry. I knew the store in Pétion-Ville would expose us to another customer in Haiti, and this was just the sort of collaboration we needed. I could not have been more excited. Then came the challenge: Cole needed the first prototype complete in two weeks. The team exchanged wide-eyed glances. This was uncharted territory for us. Until that moment, we had never taken a sketch of a conceptual design and made patterns to produce a sandal prototype; we had always worked from existing models, tweaking and perfecting them. Knowing we were out of our depth, we called upon Zaka, the great African shoemaker who lived in the neighboring community of Paco.

Zaka said he would make us patterns to produce the prototype, but with two stipulations. First, since his workshop didn't have electricity, we would need to buy gas for his generator, and second, if we expected him to work after hours, he would also require a steady flow of Prestige. We complied without hesitation. Accompanied by the hum of the generator, Sarah took on the task of sitting up all night with Zaka, drinking warm beer and watching the great shoemaker create sandal patterns in the spirit of what Cole had envisioned.

After receiving the patterns from Zaka, the team worked frantically to craft Cole's design, desperate to perfect the details. The pressure to impress Cole weighed heavily on everyone, but it also fueled our determination. And somehow, within the two-week deadline, the first prototype was complete. Since only Sarah and I have visas, we carried our precious creation to New York City to present it to Cole. Walking down the city streets of the Big Apple with our sandals in hand, we were giddy with excitement, thinking our business had really made it now. Stepping into his sleek office building we could hardly contain our nerves. As we waited for the administrative assistant to show us into the meeting room, I quietly prayed that the rest of the team could feel the weight of this moment. Then we were ushered into his office, standing face to face with Kenneth Cole. As he examined the prototype, he said a few things I will never forget.

"The world still isn't paying attention. The power of the fashion industry could change the world, and yet we do so little." It was the first time I had heard someone with real influence in the fashion world articulate this profound truth. Then, his eyes scanning the rough edges and imperfect stitching, he said, "Well, these certainly are handmade." The sandals lacked the sleek sophistication of Kenneth Cole's New York aesthetic, yet he didn't hesitate. He placed an order for his Haiti store. As delighted as I was with the order, I wanted more. I wanted him to buy our sandals for all his stores. More hesitant this time, Cole took a deep breath. Then he decided the story behind the sandals was worth showcasing in one of his New York City stores, and he doubled his order.

Two months later the day came to unveil the sandals, and Cole held nothing back. He hosted a big event at his Soho store to launch them and we were able to celebrate the newest product on his shelf, The Kenneth Cole: Love Haiti Sandals. However, the euphoria of that launch quickly gave way to the reality of our challenges. Cole's team

Port-au-Prince, Haiti. Excited by our repurposed tire sole, on his second visit to Deux Mains, Kenneth Cole spent time with us to learn our processes and observe how we manufactured our handmade sandals.

in New York had experts for every task: logistics, design, export, procurement. On our side everyone was new to the industry, and we were overwhelmed. It was a whirlwind of deadlines and problem-solving, a storm so consuming that we couldn't rise to the challenge. It proved that no matter how dedicated we were to this partnership, we needed more support and guidance than Cole and his team could offer. The dream of taking the world by storm felt increasingly out of reach. I began to learn the hard truth that the fashion industry does not thrive on slow development. Perfection is the currency here, and anything less is unacceptable. Although I prayed for this to be the collaboration that took Deux Mains to a new level, in the end our sandal orders began to decrease, and the relationship began to fade. I was crushed, disappointed at my incomplete understanding of the market, and I replayed my shortcomings over and over in my mind.

I had placed so much hope in the collaboration with Cole, but the more we were thrust into the world of fashion and consumerism, the more it became clear that we still hadn't found our niche. The year was ending in a dark place, where it seemed we weren't good enough for some of the Christian customers we had in Haiti, nor were we good enough to produce for big designers globally. I was facing another crossroads in this journey, and in that moment of uncertainty, clarity emerged. The path forward wasn't about trying to please either audience. It was about seeing beyond Western opinions and recognizing the brilliance in the local talent all around me, so the next time an opportunity like Kenneth Cole came knocking on our door, we would be ready by ensuring that what made us unique—the incredible craft and creativity of Haiti itself—shone brightly enough for any customer. I needed to stop looking for validation or an outside savior; instead I needed to cultivate what was already growing on our own soil.

I wasn't the only one who took failed partnerships to heart. The team also felt them deeply, but it was together that we decided to look inward and focus on the artistry that was already alive on the island. In Port-au-Prince the leatherworking community is small, a tight-knit group where everyone knows each other. One morning Jolina leaned over to me and said, "I just met a man downtown who sells leather to craftspeople in the area. He's well-connected and could be a good lead to find the new talent you are looking for." Powered with Jolina's new contact we put out a call, hoping the right person would hear that Deux Mains was searching for artists in the city. By midday the word had spread like wildfire, eventually reaching Emmanuel, a master craftsperson from Carrefour. Emmanuel wasn't just skilled; he was legendary. His stall on Avenue John Brown was one of the most sought-after spots in Port-au-Prince, a place where shoppers marveled at the beauty of his handmade leather goods. Emmanuel didn't necessarily need another job; his stall provided well for his family. But curiosity got the better of him, and he decided to visit the workshop and see what we were all about.

Emmanuel, not only a talented artisan but a family man, was equally invested in his children's gifts. He noticed early on that his eldest son Michel had a natural talent, shaping leather with the kind of ease and elegance that couldn't be taught. Michel had served as Emmanuel's apprentice for years. Now he was a new high school graduate preparing for his next step in life. He loved the art form and was eager to see our factory as well, so his father agreed they could make the trek from their hometown of Carrefour together. Carrefour, with its intricate web of scattered settlements and bustling streets, is seventeen kilometers southwest of downtown Port-au-Prince. Overcrowding and poverty shaped the daily fabric of life, but the growing shadow of organized gangs made it especially dangerous. Father and son took the trip to the city center carefully, and when they arrived at the workshop, all eyes were on Emmanuel. He approached the craft test with modest confidence. Michel watched his father sew pieces of leather together on our motorized machine, skiving edges of the material with total ease and assembling the pieces like a true master. When he had completed the test, Emmanuel wiped the sweat from his brow, stood up, and followed Jolina back to her office. After a few moments of banter, Emmanuel shook his head with a polite smile.

"Thank you," he said, "but I have decided I can't leave my stall." And with that he turned to leave, Michel only a few steps behind him. They had just made it past the factory walls when Michel stopped to ask his father, "Can I take the test?"

Emmanuel looked at him, perplexed. Michel had never used a motorized sewing machine before; he had worked only on a manual pedal machine. However, believing that his son was destined for great things, and more importantly understanding the worsening climate of their hometown community, where the gangs were starting to formalize and targeting young men such as Michel, Emmanuel agreed. He knew the only way to avoid interactions with the gangs was to stay out of their path, and being nineteen Michel would be a prime target for them. Emmanuel reasoned that if there was a job for Michel here, it could be a way to save him from the gangs that would eventually come knocking on the door.

They turned back to the gates of the Deux Mains factory where Jolina, surprised but excited, walked Michel to the sewing machine to take the test. She watched closely, secretly hoping Michel would impress her as much as his father had. The leather moved through Michel's hands with grace and precision. Neither Michel nor his father could believe his natural abilities on this machine, but stitch by stitch he proved that his gift was real. The same genius that lived in his father had been passed down to him. Jolina was delighted. Emmanuel and Michel exchanged a look of quiet joy, knowing something extraordinary had just taken place.

A few days later Michel signed a contract to work at Deux Mains. With his sense of imagination, he was perfect for designing the latest handbag collections, and his patient mentorship inspired others to greatness, guiding Deux Mains to become a brand desired by fashion connoisseurs around the world. More than his investment in our fashion side, Michel's steady commitment has always been a source of strength for me, and many times I've drawn on his example. It was in his faith that I uncovered what the connection between my spirituality and the fashion world we were building meant to me. He knew I struggled when those piercing questions about our business not being Christian enough came, but then one day he helped me understand: it's not about me, or whether our team can pass some spiritual litmus test. The real question is simpler. How are we showing our values to the consumers we do encounter, whether missionary or fashionista, and how can we help encourage more intentional buying practices to make the world a better, safer place for all families?

His insight was a revolutionary force on the way I saw my position in the fight for economic freedom, because I realized it is the everyday consumers who control the flow of money. Therefore, it is with the buyers of the world that our responsibility lies. I dove into what the Bible had to say and was surprised to find more than 2,000 verses about finances and possessions. This told me God cares deeply about how we handle our finances, especially in places like Haiti where money can be the deciding factor in whether a family stays together or falls apart. Michel was right. If we are rooted in our beliefs, then our spending habits should reflect our values. I started to imagine what the world could look like if the 2.4 billion Christians around the world spent their money on items made in fair trade factories without slave labor, or on slow-fashion pieces that didn't harm the environment. That sort of purchasing power would change the world, and Deux Mains could be a part of that. I decided that instead of trying to choose between faith and fashion, and succumbing to the judgments of others, I could shift my attitude about the position I was in. This was how we could use our business to help build a world with more equity and justice for all people. This was why we had to continue to grow the brand and focus our energy on all types of customers who came into our community.

CHAPTER 14

REMEMBER, RISE, AND REBUILD

Let us not be satisfied with a mediocre life.
Pope Francis

○

The weekend of January 12, 2018, marked a somber anniversary. For the eighth year in a row, the world remembered the ruthless earthquake that claimed more than 250,000 lives. Front-page news reports once again marveled that 1.5 million people had become homeless overnight and billions of aid dollars had seemed to mysteriously vanish. But we chose a different path. Instead of solely grieving, we organized a weekend tribute to remember those who had lost their lives, and also to celebrate the tenacity of the survivors. To accomplish this, we were going to reveal to the world the new factory we had built. Months of meticulous preparation had led to this three-day event.

We called it "Remember, Rise, and Rebuild," and our homage was set to begin with the unveiling of the new Deux Mains factory. This debut was about more than opening a

2018 New Solar Powered Deux Mains factory, Port-au-Prince, Haiti. We started the year with an empty space and within months filled this new space, 11 times larger than our previous one, to scale our company and abilities—hiring more Haitian craftspeople and shoemakers, making an even larger impact.

new manufacturing center; it was about showcasing innovation in a beautiful space born from abandoned ruins. The walls, freshly painted, bore no trace of the damage they had once sustained. Now they were alive with the promise of what could be. Eleven times larger than our previous shop, with worktables dedicated to artisanal craft and solar panels shining on the rooftop, this factory intentionally blended old and new. It embodied all the fair-trade and sustainability principles we held so dear. And it wasn't just ours; it belonged to every person who believed in Haiti's ability to rise above the rubble and dream of an economically free nation.

When the official ribbon-cutting day arrived, the factory was alive with anticipation. A talented troubadour band was in full swing, and attendees danced around the tables and machines. The mayor of our neighborhood, well-respected friends in the community, and other special dignitaries each spoke eloquently about what businesses based in Haiti meant for people and the economy. Guests marveled at the authentic dishes served that highlighted the vibrant flavors of the island, and they toasted each other with Haiti's iconic dark rum, which flowed freely.

Among the crowd, a woman moved quietly through the room. Suzanne, an American who had come to Haiti years earlier to run a nonprofit focused on education, Bridge Scholarship, had fallen in love with the country, and visited often. She strolled around the factory with curiosity, taking it all in, the skillful hands of the craftspeople hard at work demonstrating their talent, the polished machines standing alongside hand-sewn bags and sandals on display, the vibrant energy of a dream made real. Her demeanor was serene, but the spark of curiosity and admiration in her eyes was hard to miss. Suzanne wasn't just any guest. She carried with her an energy, a presence that suggested she was here for something bigger.

As the daughter of a hedge fund manager, Suzanne had long harbored dreams of not just working with nonprofits but also using her resources to invest in businesses that created meaningful change. Standing in the heart of the new Deux Mains factory, a space filled with promise and purpose, she heard the Lord say, "If not us, then who?" and she instantly knew her role in the story was just beginning. She soon became our first private investor, a believer not just in Deux Mains but in the power of business in Haiti itself.

Suzanne's role as a private investor marked a turning point for me as a leader and forever altered the trajectory of our business. Suzanne understood the complexities and the often-messy realities of doing business in a country shaped by hardship, and unlike traditional investment goals, which measure success solely by profit, her approach was different. It was financing in the form of an impact investment, designed to blend financial goals with the humanitarian and environmental mission that defined Deux Mains.

Suzanne's belief in our purpose gave me freedom I hadn't felt before to speak openly about the financial pressures and operational obstacles we faced that were unique to Haiti. Her investment wasn't just an injection of cash; it was the foundation of a shared understanding about how to make an impact investment succeed in one of the most challenging environments in the Western Hemisphere. Suzanne listened, and then she began to unlock new opportunities for us. Slowly but surely, the ripple effect of her faith in Deux

Mains began to expand beyond Haiti. Her advocacy attracted two more believers: Tom and Paul, investors who shared her vision for a business that could thrive in Haiti while uplifting its people.

Even though neither had visited Haiti, Tom and Paul were eager to see the country healthy and economically strong. Impact investing was in Tom's blood, so with a family legacy of using capital to create positive change, he rigorously challenged me on our finances before committing. His thoroughness wasn't intimidating, however; it was empowering, and it pushed me to refine my vision and sharpen my goals. Paul, on the other hand, was new to impact investing. He brought a talent for navigating the unpredictability of business in the developing world. His ability to work through tough scenarios was endless, and with his careful, measured approach, he meticulously examined the numbers and patiently worked with us to develop a plan that was grounded in reality. Together, Suzanne, Tom, and Paul became more than investors; they became mentors and partners in a vision far greater than any of us could achieve alone.

Not long after our new partnership was established, travel disruptions and escalating violence in Haiti meant things were about to become rocky for us again. Our boutique, which had been our lifeline, began to suffer. I remember standing in that shop, watching the flow of visitors slow to a trickle, and feeling the weight of uncertainty settle in. But in that struggle, we discovered something undeniable: when people could touch our bags, feel the leather, and see the craftsmanship with their own eyes, they connected in a way that no photograph online could ever capture.

That realization inspired our next move. I knew we couldn't rely on waiting for people to come to Haiti, we had to bring Haiti to them, physically. It was then that I decided to turned my attention to small boutique buyers abroad, shop owners who could introduce our work to customers face to face. What felt at first like another loss slowly revealed itself as a lesson. Our survival, and our growth, depended on creating those moments of physical connection, even if they happened far from the island. With the trio's guidance, and for the first time in Deux Mains' history, we didn't have to rely on good fortune and luck; we had the resources to alter our plans and to think like a growing fashion brand.

I found clarity in the challenge, but once again I was operating in the unknown. I had to begin the process of branding and marketing with the sophistication and reach needed to bridge the gap between our Haitian roots and a wholesale customer base on other continents. It was something I had been praying about for years. "How, God, with all we have to manage here in Haiti, would it be possible to focus on what customers across the world need?"

My new investors challenged me to think bigger and hold more tightly to my faith, believing the world was ready to hear our story. With their help, we began to share the heart of Deux Mains with the buyers of the world. We told the story of a factory powered by the Caribbean sun, where every product was crafted with care and purpose by Haitian artisans earning a fair wage. We offered customers not just fashion but the chance to be part of something meant to create change. Would the world respond the way we hoped? As I set my sights on using our business to help redefine the fashion industry, I realized I was up against some very powerful adversaries. We had to take on a business sector that, at its core, thrives on exploitation, relying on slave labor, environmental destruction, and a disposable mindset sold to the masses as "trendy."

But I still believed there was a segment of consumers and small businesses out there that wanted something better. People searching for fashion that aligned with their values, pieces that weren't just beautiful but carried a story of sustainability, fair wages, and hope. We developed an ambitious plan: attend dozens of trade shows in the United States and Canada, bringing our handbags and sandals to the world. I envisioned Deux Mains accessories displayed in boutique windows and the most stylish department stores.

The plan was solid, the energy electric. But just as we were ready to soar, the world caught fire. News of an infectious disease caused by the SARS-CoV-2 virus spread like a shadow over the globe. One by one, trade shows were canceled. Flights were grounded. Borders slammed shut. Our dream, so close to becoming a reality, slipped totally out of reach and the momentum we'd worked so hard to build came to a grinding halt. The whole world seemed to pause, but for us the stakes only grew higher.

Sarah and I have weathered countless storms, both literal and figurative, in our fight to build a meaningful enterprise. But the arrival of COVID-19 was like nothing we'd faced before. Haiti was scathed by the economic devastation of the pandemic, and our business suffered greatly. Almost overnight our retail sales plummeted, our plan to reach wholesale buyers was completely halted, and when travel restrictions locked down the island, our little boutique was forced to close. It was agonizing to turn the key and lock the boutique door for what felt like the last time, knowing how we had fought to keep the doors open.

Online shopping took on a whole new meaning during this time, but even that lifeline slipped from our grasp. We didn't have the means to compete for advertising space on platforms we'd previously used. Our brand's visibility faded in the crowded online marketplace, and our sales began to tank. I could see the storm coming, but I didn't know how to steer us out of its path. Every decision I made seemed to lead us further into trouble. I began to question everything: Had I been foolish to dream this big? Had all the years of blood, sweat, and tears been for nothing? How were we supposed to keep going when it felt like the world itself was shutting down? In addition to the financial blows we were enduring, the reality of life in Port-au-Prince made the pandemic's challenges even more staggering.

A city built for no more than 150,000 people had grown to hold nearly three million, making the luxury of social distancing impossible for most Haitians. Daily life unfolded in cramped, congested places, and there was no viable solution. At the factory, we followed the government mandates, working at only 30 percent capacity and leaving 70 percent of our team without access to work for months. It was devastating to send them home knowing there were no safety nets to catch them. Even though we pay high taxes in Haiti, there was not one relief program or government subsidy available to us to help with the loss of income due to the pandemic. Every action we took to protect our business and our team came about through our own creativity and financial resources.

Billy and I immediately called upon the donors, clients, and relationships we had built over the years in the United States, the UK, and Haiti. Using social media to our advantage, we described the Haitian pandemic experience to the world, and despite their own suffering, people stepped up again. Generous donations poured in, allowing us to create our own furlough system. We were able to pay team members who were temporarily forced out of jobs, ensuring they could rely on their paycheck despite the newest challenge we now faced. Those still working in the factory pivoted overnight. Instead of making high-end handbags, we began producing facemasks for hospitals and other non-governmental organizations (NGOs) working across Haiti. We did whatever it took to stay afloat, but only barely, and only because of the generosity of the community that we built. Thanks to outside investment in our business, we were also able to build a hand-washing station in the factory and pay for motos, so our craftspeople didn't have to ride crowded tap-taps to work. COVID-19 nearly broke us, but it also revealed the best in people who went out of their way to help us keep our team safe.

The team in Haiti also honed their own grit and stamina to survive the effects of the pandemic. After the mask contracts were finished, we had to think fast and adjust our business model again and again, grabbing hold of any faint opportunity that presented itself. It was a time of constant reinvention, and I knew that smart collaborations could give us the boost we needed. That's when I had the idea to create our newest venture, a collaboration with my husband.

Billy's military career had set him up to do many things in the world, and one of those happened to be appearing on television. Billy was in the cast of *SAS: Who Dares Wins*, a popular UK reality show inspired by the Special Forces selection process that takes celebrities and civilians through a physically and mentally demanding ten-day training course. The show deeply resonated with me because it showed the humanity of each contestant, a reminder that as human beings we all suffer, but when we work together, we can accomplish anything.

Several years ago, the show had caught even wider attention, and my husband was thrust into the international spotlight. It was the kind of moment that happens only once in a lifetime, and before we knew it, Billy was boarding a plane to Australia with his team to recreate the show for an Australian fan base. The program was an undeniable success, and soon it made its way to the States, rebranded as *Special Forces: World's Toughest Test*. Through our years together, Billy had transformed from a mysterious soldier who opened up about his military experiences only when he and his friends swapped war stories over too many drinks, into a man whose heroic tales were being told in books, magazines, and national television broadcasts. It has been quite the transition for our family, but Billy always used his position to help others, and this time was no exception. As his success grew, he wanted to shine a light back on Haiti.

Loving my work and watching me build this brand has always inspired Billy. He appreciated that Deux Mains products were mostly for women, but he challenged me to be more inclusive, to bridge the gap between the women's collection we had, and the men's market we had yet to tap into.

Sitting across from him one evening, I asked, "As a man, what do you want from a brand like ours?" Billy's response was simple. "I want leather goods that make sense for a man who travels a lot, things that will make my life easier."

Billy's new world was one of constant travel, and he wanted to carry Deux Mains with him, so we started brainstorming. His military background taught him to seek out practical, durable gear that could withstand the test of time, and with our expertise in luxury leather, why not create a high-end leather travel line that could capture the same sense of rugged sophistication he lived by? We spent the next year developing a travel line that merged luxury with Billy's military precision to capture a new client base. The idea wasn't just to create beautiful and functional leather goods, but also to appeal to the modern man who valued both style and durability.

And so, in coordination with Billy's new show in the United States, a new collection from Deux Mains would follow. It was the perfect marriage of opportunity and passion. We were eager to embrace this new opportunity. Yet as the consequences of COVID started to diminish, another turning point in Haiti's history gave us one more unprecedented challenge to overcome. The same day we were scheduled to fly in for a photoshoot to capture our new collaboration collection, Sarah was jolted awake by a commotion in her front yard. With sleep still in her eyes, she stumbled to her front door and joined the small group of neighbors speaking in anxious tones, their faces etched with disbelief and sorrow. Hours earlier, gunmen had burst into the Port-au-Prince home of Haitian President Jovenel Moïse, killing him and critically injuring his wife. Regardless of people's different opinions of the president's capacity or political effectiveness, the population was united in horror.

Sarah called me immediately, her voice unrecognizable as she related the details coming to light. She had heard that the killers weren't locals; they were foreign mercenaries, a chilling reminder of the fragility of Haiti's sovereignty. At home in Florida, I grew terrified as I listened to her. The political situation was unraveling rapidly, and the assassination had created a threat to everyone in the country.

"You need to evacuate," I told Sarah urgently, thinking of her safety and that of the guests from the United States who were staying at her home. We had no idea what events might follow. The murder of Haiti's head of state spat in the face of hopes for the country's peaceful, democratic future, and I feared the worst.

Despite my apprehension, I took some deep breaths and calmed down, knowing we needed to see what happened next before we made any drastic moves. In the meantime, Sarah ventured to the corner store in her neighborhood to buy food and water in preparation for a potential lockdown if we decided she and her guests could stay. The streets were eerily quiet, as if the entire country were holding its breath. A few people sat on their front steps, staring into the distance with eyes glazed over and listening to radio reporters discussing Haiti's uncertain future in voices filled with unease. Walking by them, Sarah felt uncomfortable. Haiti's painful history of colonization by our ancestors, a legacy of economic embargoes, and foreign interference that crippled the nation ran through her mind as the radios crackled. The latest reports suggested that at least one of the killers was American. Yet the people she passed greeted her only with soft, sad smiles.

With no clear line of succession, Haiti became wracked by political uncertainty, and in the power vacuum that followed, violent gangs flourished, not just in known gang areas, but all around Port-au-Prince. In a matter of months, they began running the city. Schools, businesses, and the routines of everyday life were thrown into disarray, and once-vibrant streets became places of fear and uncertainty. Residents found themselves trapped in a cycle of violence, with clashes between rival gangs erupting on a daily basis. Frequent reports of kidnappings and extortion filled the news and stripped people of any sense of safety. Access to necessities such as food, water, and medical supplies was severely restricted, exacerbating the already dire humanitarian situation. The control exerted by gangs also hindered economic activity, leaving many struggling to make ends meet and causing a decline in overall living standards. Our business would not be immune to the turmoil, and I knew we couldn't just sit back and wait for things to get worse.

We had no clear answers, no guarantees, but we had to do everything in our power to ensure the safety of the company and the team. It seemed as if every day brought a new layer of fear. Michel no longer needed to commute from Carrefour through the notoriously dangerous Martissant area, but now he faced constant peril traveling the short distance from his new home to the factory. Threatened daily, caught between overworked police and violent gangs, he said it was like living in hell, a place thick with fear where everyone is afraid of each other.

As I listened to his words, I couldn't help but imagine what it is like to live in that constant state of anxiety. The community was being tested in so many ways. The sounds of gunfire in the distance, the murmurs of danger on every corner, were more than just a threat to physical safety. They were a threat to people's very way of life. As a business owner, I struggled to know what were the right choices to make. Should the team make the dangerous trek to work each morning? Should we succumb to the gangs and close our business? Should we finally give up entirely? Every day I wrestled with the same agonizing questions.

By October 2022, after weeks of endless discussions and many sleepless nights, I had made the impossible decision to temporarily close the factory. I knew there would be costly repercussions, but I thought this was the right thing to do. It wasn't until ten days later that the leadership team in Haiti decided we needed to have a serious discussion. In that pivotal meeting I realized I could not make decisions that would affect hundreds of people's lives from the safety of my home 700 miles away. The local leadership team had to decide when it was right for the factory to be open and when it was too dangerous. Their voices and their choices had to guide us. Anxiety loomed, but the team was determined to reopen the factory immediately. It was a hard choice, but the right one. We carried on producing, developing more prototypes, and creating the new lines of business we intended. We were desperate to change the narrative from the insecurity the news outlets seemed solely interested in broadcasting, to the artistry and talent that Haiti has to offer. We wanted to remind people of the humanity that was still alive on the island.

CHAPTER 15

MOTHERHOOD

Let everything happen to you. Beauty and
Terror. Just keep going. No feeling is final.
Rainer Maria Rilke

○

Since their inception, I have been obsessed with Deux Mains and REBUILD globally, and work often took the driver's seat in my life. The tug-of-war between career demands and personal aspirations has been constant, and I'll be the first to admit I haven't always found the right balance. Each morning began with crisis management, each evening ended with exhaustion, and the space between was filled with impossible decisions. But there was another part of me coming to the surface, a quieter but no less powerful part, that yearned to become a mother.

After Billy and I were married, we began our quest to start a family together. I pictured myself the proud matriarch of a little tribe of global humanitarians, my babies tied to my back as I trampled dusty roads of underdeveloped communities, speaking to other mothers more skilled than I.

It never occurred to me that it might not happen. I believed motherhood was something that would just naturally come, or that I could achieve it with sheer will and determination, just as I had done with so many other things in life. But that isn't how our story goes. Instead, the reality of infertility blindsided me. Over the years, my hopelessness had usually been about the conditions of Haiti, or the injustice women and girls everywhere face, issues that are monumental and deeply personal to me. But this? Not being able to rely on my own body, not being able to make a family, felt like the ultimate betrayal. It was a new, very private, all-consuming level of hell.

When my doctors told me that reducing stress might help me conceive, I wasn't sure whether to laugh or cry. I was running a fashion company in Haiti during one of its most tumultuous times, and stress was practically embedded in my DNA. But I wanted to become a mother so desperately that I decided to give it my all. With the steady support of Billy and my team, I spent nearly two years learning to calm myself, focus, and breathe. I began a weekly self-care routine, going to acupuncture and even finding a yoga guru on YouTube who became my virtual guide each morning. Despite my efforts, however, the three rounds of IVF I endured were heartbreaking, each failure more crushing than the last. Hollowed by disappointment, I walked around like a zombie, overwhelmed by feelings of worthlessness. Billy tried everything he could think of to help me heal. In the months that followed he'd remind me of all the amazing things we had in our life, of the love we shared, of the impact of our work in Haiti. Nothing he said could penetrate my sadness. His final attempt was to break me out of every comfort zone boundary I had, believing that if I faced other issues that caused me angst, I might begin to heal.

In pursuit of this goal, Billy first thought I should conquer my paralyzing fear of heights. Before joining the SAS, he had been in the parachute regiment, spending most of his formative years jumping out of planes. He loved floating through the air, weightless and free. He found a local skydiving school and tried to convince me to join him. As a former professional aerialist, I considered that hanging from a chiffon scarf forty feet in the air was enough of a challenge. Skydiving seemed reckless and utterly unnecessary. I refused every invitation, determined to keep my feet firmly planted on solid ground. But somehow, in early December 2023, I found myself strapped to a complete stranger at 18,000 feet in the air. As we catapulted out of the plane, I momentarily lost consciousness from the shock of the free fall, but I was quickly awakened by the freezing cold rain cloud we were dropping through at maximum speed. I immediately thought this is what it must feel like to be waterboarded. I couldn't breathe. But then the parachute opened and the frantic rush slowed. We soared through the air and I felt a peace come over me. The world was so much bigger and more beautiful from up in the sky.

Billy's unconventional therapy didn't stop there. For my birthday, he arranged for me to take a flying lesson in a tiny plane, a feat that seemed even more impossible than skydiving. He knew I deeply feared those little planes and would never fly in one. I hated them so much that I had refused to board one to deliver medication to earthquake survivors in the early days of the Haitian disaster. But Billy was persistent, and I found myself climbing into the cockpit of that miniature aircraft, my legs shaking as I stepped into the claustrophobic space next to the pilot. I muttered a Hail Mary under my breath, convinced there was no way this toy plane would have the strength to carry us into the clouds. I had my eyes shut tight as we took off, bracing for the worst. But when I finally opened them, we were sailing over the everglades of South Florida. The marshes shimmered in the sunlight and I felt myself releasing the tension and pain I had been holding onto for so long.

Although these activities were never on my bucket list, Billy believed that with each fear I defeated, I would once again believe in us, and in our ability to overcome anything. His plan was working. Each terror I faced chipped away at the wall of despair I had built around myself. I started to find myself again, and with time I found peace, not just with our losses but with the life we already had. I began to once again see the beauty in our little family: my steadfast husband, my courageous stepchildren, and our bulldog Alfie.

A few days after Christmas, life threw us the most unexpected shock. During my mammogram appointment, an unremarkable annual task on my to-do list, something happened that I never believed possible. As I sat in the sterile waiting room, flipping through the usual medical forms, I reached the page where the practitioner asks you to confirm you're not pregnant. A bizarre feeling crept over me. I stared at the words, pen hovering, and just couldn't bring myself to sign it. Sheepishly I walked to the receptionist, gripping the clipboard.

"I'm really sorry," I began, feeling foolish, "but I feel like I can't sign this paper."

She looked at me a bit perplexed and asked, "Are you pregnant?"

"No," I sighed, shaking my head, oversharing about my infertility troubles and years of hopelessness.

Her expression softened and she gently said, "Well, ma'am, if you don't sign the paper, we can't allow you to have your mammogram." I shuffled back to the bright orange seat to finish my paperwork, feeling ridiculous. But no matter how many times I flipped the papers back and forth, I just couldn't sign. My heart was racing as I walked back to the reception desk.

"I'm so sorry," I whispered, "but I just can't sign it."

She took the clipboard from my hands and suggested, "How about we do a quick pregnancy test, just to be sure?"

I let out a nervous laugh, waving my hand dismissively. "Sure, go ahead," I said, already bracing for disappointment. "It'll be the same as the hundred other tests I've taken."

Ten minutes later, my legs buckled and I fell to my knees in the bathroom of the doctor's office, staring in disbelief at the two beautiful strong pink lines that ran across the tiny window of the pregnancy test. Tears blurred my vision as I crawled toward the door, fumbling to unlock it.

"I'm pregnant!" I screamed, holding the test aloft like a trophy. Between hugs and tears, I begged the nurses to tell me it was true.

The receptionist took my hands and said, "How about I call your OB-GYN, and you take one more test just to be sure?" Another test, same result: two beautiful symmetric pink lines confirming the impossible.

On the way home I called Billy, trying to keep my voice steady. "Hey, could you leave lunch with the guys and meet me at home?" I asked awkwardly.

"What's going on? Are you okay?" he asked, concerned. The weight of my silence must have sent him into a spin, but I assured him I was fine. I spent the rest of the drive in utter shock. By the time I got home, I was pacing the hallway, cycling through every cute Pinterest-worthy idea, trying to find the perfect words to tell him we were pregnant.

When Billy finally burst through the door, eyes wide with worry, he asked again, "What's wrong?" It took a second for me to realize what he must have been thinking, but still no words would come out of my mouth. Leaving the front door open behind him, he stepped closer, put his hands on my shoulders, and stared into my eyes. "Jules, what is going on?"

I had dreamed of this moment for so long, and when I opened my mouth all my well-rehearsed words dissolved into a jumble. "We're ... I'm ... we're ..." I stuttered, my heart pounding louder than my thoughts. And then in perfect unison we both blurted out, "PREGNANT!"

We spent the next three months in total bliss. We loved everything about being pregnant. I suffered from horrendous morning sickness, but instead of resenting it, I found it comforting, a daily reminder of the little life growing inside me. I experimented with every form of ginger to help with the nausea, and I loved finding ways to incorporate it into my rapidly changing diet. It didn't take long for my thin frame to adapt to the demands of pregnancy, almost immediately gaining twenty-two pounds. But no matter how tight my jeans became, I embraced the feeling, enjoying every moment on the couch cuddling with my little pot belly. Billy, however, refused to let me slow down. Despite my protests, he would push me to walk over the rolling Malvern hills near our home in the UK I felt tired just looking at them, but no matter how exhausted I said I was, he insisted that we walk. In preparation I would unbutton my pants, he'd bend over to double-knot my shoelaces, and then he led the way.

As we walked, the cool air blew over our faces and I enjoyed the moments of quiet reflection. I started sketching ideas for baby bags and mommy-and-me sandals, imagining how I could weave this new chapter of my life into my work. I also dreamed of inspiring other women with our story of struggle, figuring out ways I could be sensitive yet uplifting to women who also dreamed of motherhood. But before I had the chance to flesh out this dream, our joy came to a chilling halt. At our fifteen-week scan, the technician's face grew solemn as he told us to wait for the doctor to come in. Minutes later we learned that our baby had stopped growing and no longer had a heartbeat.

I felt the life fall out of me and a deep emptiness reached into the core of my soul. The weeks and months that followed were some of the darkest in my life. It was a long time before I felt anything other than grief. But as we always had, Billy and I leaned on each other. We stuck together, carried on believing in each other, and refused to let the anguish define us. Eventually we found peace in the loss of our baby. I'm not sure I will ever feel whole again, but I constantly tell myself, *We're all just people. We all have terrible things that happen to us in life. Hopefully, we all have wonderful things happen to us, too.*

The love of my family and friends while I worked through the devastating loss held me up when I could no longer stand. And as grateful as I was to each of them, there was only one place in the world I wanted to be after my miscarriage. I wanted to be in Haiti and spend some time surrounded by the team. As difficult as the small and complicated island is, it's also my sanctuary. It's in Haiti that I feel most alive and most connected to something bigger than myself. Maybe the reason is that Haiti is where I birthed an organization and a business, or maybe it's that the spirit of my Haitian colleagues is so determined and strong. I craved that strength, and I needed to be immersed in something I felt I had done right.

The flight to Haiti after my miscarriage was unusually quiet, not because the hum of the engines dimmed or the murmurs of passengers were softer than usual, but because I didn't say a single word to anyone. I stared out the window, watching the clouds roll by as I tried to piece together how life had pulled me under like a riptide. When I arrived in Port-au-Prince, I barely noticed the blazing sun, relentless in its heat. I just stepped in a taxi, let the city blur past me, and drove straight to the factory. When I arrived, I felt so distant, like I was living behind a pane of glass. But I carried on up the stairs and into the open space. The air smelled of leather and sawdust, familiar and grounding. I scanned the room, looking past all the artisans cutting and sewing, and my eyes landed on him, a tall young man in the middle of the room.

Rooston was sitting at the head of the jewelry table, hunched over his work with a tranquil intensity. I walked straight to him and he looked up, his expression softening when he saw me. He started to rise, but before he was upright I fell into his arms, sobbing uncontrollably. He never asked me what was wrong; he just held me until I stopped crying, never saying a word.

Rooston isn't just a success story from REBUILD globally and the Deux Mains Academy; he is family. From the moment we met many years earlier, I felt a special connection to him—a young boy who endured more pain than any child should. Rooston's mother had died during childbirth, and he lost his father in the earthquake. The day I met him he had a fresh scar on his face from the blade of another street child he'd had a disagreement with. Even at a young age, Rooston was tall like me, and I couldn't help but imagine that if I had a child, they would be as tall as he. I admired his muted strength, yet I always felt an overwhelming urge to protect him. When he got older, the hardships of his life weighed heavily on him and he carried a lot of anger. But with me, the anger never showed. He never resented me for what I couldn't give him or what he didn't have. Rooston just loved me back. And after years of hard work and training, this talented young man had beaten all the odds to become the head jewelry maker at Deux Mains.

When my tears eased, Rooston walked me into Jolina's office, where the space felt normal and comfortable. Jolina rose slowly but didn't hesitate to hold me up by my arms. She stared straight into my eyes and said, "I lost a baby once," and with a reassuring nod she wiped my tears and told me never to lose my faith. Minouche, one of Jolina's closest friends and our trusted colleague, saw our exchange through the glass window and came into the office. She told us she too had suffered a miscarriage, and then she lowered her head to let me know it was time to move on. After a few moments of silence, we all went to work.

As much as I found purpose in my work at the factory, allowing its endless demands to keep the darkest corners of my mind occupied, Sarah saw through me. She sensed the despair lingering just beneath the surface. Work alone wasn't enough to heal me, and she knew it. One evening, as the sun dipped low over Port-au-Prince, she turned to me with a knowing smile and said, "You need to see my favorite place in Haiti."

The next day, as soon as we closed the factory gates, we rented a car and headed north to Cap-Haïtien, the city Sarah swore would soothe my soul. The drive was long, the roads winding through landscapes that shifted from bustling streets to serene, untouched wilderness. The journey began with hope and anticipation but quickly turned into a test of patience.

About two hours into the drive, Sarah announced, "We're stopping in Gonaïves. Trust me, you'll love it." We pulled into a rocky side street and stepped into a tiny apothecary, its air thick with the sweet, fermented scent of sugarcane. The owner poured us each a small cup of Clairin, a fiery, unfiltered spirit that burned going down but left a warmth that lingered. Sarah grinned, raising her cup. "To adventure!" she toasted. We downed the Clairin, its raw, earthy flavor jolting us with energy. Moments later, Kesha was blasting from the car speakers as we sped away, singing at the top of our lungs and letting the music dissolve the miles ahead.

The scenery as we drove north was beautiful. To our left, the beach stretched endlessly, waves lapping against the shore, while the mountains on our right rose sharply, commanding attention. It was breathtaking, but the road told a different story. Potholes cratered every stretch, and the little manual Rav4 bucked and bounced with every hit. Sarah cursed under her breath as she navigated the worst patches, her knuckles white while clenching the steering wheel. I was agitated, my back on fire. But slowly, the air began to feel different, lighter, freer, and when we arrived, all the discomfort melted away. We pulled into the parking lot of Mont Joli, a charming gingerbread-style hotel overlooking the city. It became our refuge for the next three days as we explored the region's historical treasures, soaking in the raw beauty and resilient spirit of its people. Despite the sadness I carried, Haiti's powerful history breathed life back into me.

Cap-Haïtien unfolded like a storybook. Its noble ruins and deep history brought life into the surrounding hills. Sarah's voice brimmed with excitement as she described our first destination: the Citadelle. This grand fortress, she explained, was a marvel of human perseverance and pride. It had taken thirteen years and the labor of more than 200,000 formerly enslaved people to build, its towering walls standing as both a symbol of defiance and a practical shield against future colonizers. When we arrived, its sheer magnitude left me breathless. The maze of walls and corridors seemed endless, each stone whispering tales of Haiti's fight for freedom. Standing inside the Citadelle's cold stone walls, I reflected on the extraordinary resilience of the Haitian people. Here, in the very place where enslaved people had overthrown their oppressors in 1804, I felt the pulse of human courage. Led by Toussaint L'Ouverture, Haiti's revolution was the only successful slave-led revolt in history. It ended slavery in Haiti nearly sixty years before emancipation in the United States, shattering the chains of colonizers without help from any other nation.

Yet Haiti's victory came at a cost. The vanquished French demanded reparations for their loss of enslaved people and property, payments that bled Haiti dry for more than a century. By the late 1800s, Haitian farmers couldn't even eat their own crops as exports fed the demands of France. The US occupation from 1915 to 1934 brought further exploitation, with unfair trade policies and martial law impoverishing the Haitian people while US banks and businesses profited. With each layer of oppression, Haiti's fight for freedom only grew more extraordinary. Its people endured centuries of brutality, from Spanish colonization to French plantation rule, when it was cheaper to replace enslaved workers than care for them. Yet they never surrendered their dignity. Walking those sacred grounds, I understood Haiti's history not just as a series of events but as a testament to the indomitable human spirit. Despite everything, the Haitian people refused to be broken.

Just a few miles from the Citadelle, nestled among jungle-covered mountains, stood the ruins of the Palace of Sans Souci. If the Citadelle was Haiti's sword, Sans Souci was its heart. This was where the dream of independence had taken form, where the Haitian Revolution had first found its footing. The palace's decaying elegance was haunting, steeped in a mix of triumph and tragedy. I could almost hear the echoes of voices that had once filled its halls, voices of determination, sacrifice, and unyielding hope. I had known only fragments of these stories before from a visit to the Haitian History Museum in Port-au-Prince, miraculously untouched by the earthquake. The museum stood as a sentinel of Haiti's legacy, preserving the struggles and triumphs of a nation that had fought harder than most to be free. Walking through its halls had been a humbling experience, but now, amid the ruins of Cap-Haïtien, the weight of Haiti's history felt palpable. Sensing the pulse of history beneath my feet, I felt a flicker of life creep back into me. Recovering from losing our baby was going to be a personal battle I would need to find the strength to fight. I am not sure I would have had the courage had I not been given the gift of knowing Haiti's history and the people who make up this brave island.

The women particularly, known as the backbone of society, had shown me a strength I could only aspire to from day one. They taught me what kind of person I wanted to be, and it was in this moment of personal agony that I needed to hold onto everything they were teaching me. Building something good together was our war cry. For my Haitian colleagues it was a way of pushing back against a history that had tried to break them. For me, it was a way of fighting through the loss of my baby that had tried to break me.

CHAPTER 16

WALK A MILE IN OUR SHOES

> The idea that some lives matter less is the root of all that is wrong with the world.
>
> *Dr. Paul Farmer*

○

I've walked down many streets in many countries in my life, yet nothing I've seen abroad has affected the way we run our business quite like the vibrant market streets of Haiti. It was there that I was captivated by the women vendors, who control not only the households and commerce, but the supply chains as well. And yet as I spent more time in Haiti, I began to see the harsh truth they face. On the surface they move with purpose and strength, but underneath the reality is sobering. Centuries-old beliefs that women are somehow inferior have seeped into every corner of society. Despite having constitutional rights equal to those of men, these women, so essential to the economy and to their families, face systemic barriers that rob them of basic opportunities. It was hard to watch them navigate their daily lives, deserving so much more respect and support than they were given.

Even the data backed up what my heart already knew. International agencies like the United Nations Development Program (UNDP) have proven that the most effective strategy for fighting poverty is to put money directly into the hands of women. For every woman lifted out of poverty, seven others follow, because women invest in education and they save. Women don't have a knowledge or skills shortage; they have a cash shortage. The lack of finance isn't a personal failure, it's the result of centuries of discrimination embedded in the culture around them.

Jolina was no stranger to this life circumstance or to business in Haiti. She knew all too well the high stakes of losing a livelihood in a country where every dollar earned could mean the difference between survival and despair. She wasn't going to wait for men or the larger society to know her worth; she held on to the possibilities our business offered and made a bold decision for her life. One day after work, she turned to me with a big smile.

"Julie," she said, "I would like to invite you to my house."

"Sounds great. I'll meet you there after work." I replied. Then she started giving me directions. I raised an eyebrow, perplexed. "Jo, I've been to your house a hundred times; I don't need directions."

"No, Julie," she said, beaming with anticipation, "I want you to see my *new* house. The house I built for my family on land that I bought myself."

"Wait...what?" I gasped, staring at her. "You bought land? You built a new house?"

Jolina and her family outside the home she built on the land she purchased.

Jolina's pride was unmistakable as she explained. Steadfastly and without telling her husband, she had been saving a portion of her paychecks to acquire land. She knew if her husband found out how much money she was making, he would want to buy a tap-tap so he could start working again. As eager as Jolina was for him to get back on his feet, she knew that in Haiti, owning land and a home is more than a milestone; it's a foundation for a family's future. "I wanted to make my family secure," she said, her voice steady but filled with emotion. "This was the best decision for us."

When I arrived at her new house, I was speechless. It stood confidently on a small hill, simple and solid, a beautiful home that symbolized everything Jolina believed in and had worked for. As I took it all in, I couldn't help but feel overwhelmed by her strength, her foresight, and her sheer determination. She turned to me, her face glowing with accomplishment.

"Women," she said, "are the pillars of life here. If we want something to change, we must do it ourselves." I realized Jolina wasn't just talking about the house; she was talking about our company as well. She had taken control of her destiny in a way that defied societal norms and expectations, proving once again that the strength of Haitian women is unmatched.

Jolina's new home, and the strong impressions left in my mind of women working in the street markets of Haiti, reinspired me and brought my focus back to the goal of employing additional women. The hardships of the recent years had left me more passive and vulnerable than normal, but Jolina reminded me that we needed to be bold in our decisions and continue to push forward. I decided to rebrand the business entirely. We had a story of beauty, confidence, and craft we wanted to tell. Our last attempt at marketing had failed with the arrival of COVID-19 and the years of tragedy that followed, but our factory was still intact, and it was time to try again. This time, we would show the world how Deux Mains had evolved from a simple sandal company to a luxury handbag and small leather goods brand, a brand that sold not products but pieces of art that told our story. I was surrounded by bold and unapologetically brave stories rooted in Haitian tradition, and this is what needed to shine through in our brand.

To share our story of artistry, we knew our handbags had to embody our words. They needed to tell a tale of tradition and beauty. So we set off into the Haitian countryside, traveling more deeply into the heart of the island than ever before. There we discovered a centuries-old craft that took our breath away, the ancient tradition of basket weaving. The women who practiced this art were mesmerizing. With deft hands and unmatched precision, they wove palm fronds into intricate, sturdy baskets. Each weave, each knot, carried a story passed down through generations. Watching them work was like glimpsing into our own future, one woven with care, strength, and purpose.

I knew this art form would become the cornerstone of our rebrand. We returned to the factory inspired, and the team worked excitedly to integrate the weaving techniques into our designs, pairing them with the most sustainable and exquisite leathers we could find. The result was a collection that honored Haiti's rich heritage while reimagining it for the modern world. With every piece, we defied the stereotypes often associated with the island, sharing a story of strength and tradition with the world.

Yet our journey into the countryside had given us more than just a renewed sense of creativity. In the rural communities we visited, connecting with families and hearing their stories, one need rose above the rest: school shoes for their children. In a country where access to education can unlock the door to opportunity, proper footwear in the shape of formal black shoes was a simple yet essential requirement of the Haitian school uniform. Without the right shoes, parents told us, children were teased and humiliated, even barred from classrooms, and their futures slipped away with every missed day.

Of Haiti's 3.5 million children, perhaps as many as 1 million will never have access to school. Among the rest, 80% rely on charities or religious groups to cover tuition, uniforms, and supplies. Yet even with that crucial support, proper school shoes usually aren't included. To complete their uniforms, students are given used, donated sneakers and flipflops that often come from shoe drives in the United States. The shoe drive efforts revealed a well-intentioned but fundamentally flawed system—the shoes would arrive in Haiti mismatched, and most were worn out already. But nonetheless, they would be unloaded into towering piles at the port near the city center, where children scoured through them hoping to find a pair that fit. Often, however, they left with shoes that were uncomfortable, unsuitable for the climate, or worse—not acceptable footwear for school. I understood this charity initiative stemmed from kindness, but I also saw we needed to change the way children receive school shoes. If we didn't, we would continue to import the very problems that delayed the return of a stronger Haiti. It was a need we couldn't ignore, a call to action that would soon transform Deux Mains into something greater.

Nothing good has ever come out of the gang wars, and by this point gangs had taken over the ports and streets, choking off the nonprofits' and missionaries' access to their imported goods. This did, however, create an opportunity for us to solve a problem for these organizations, since they could no longer import shoes. For years we had honed the art of sandal-making for the export market. Why not make a school shoe that met the local government's uniform standards?

As the last large-scale leather manufacturer in Port-au-Prince, if we started to produce school shoes as well, we had a chance to make a double impact by ensuring kids have the right shoes, and creating more jobs. This new opportunity could be a powerful movement for the long-term development of the country, empowering the local economy by keeping production dollars circulating within it. I knew the old-fashioned shoe drives were never intended to hurt anyone, and in the past there may not have been another way to get shoes on children's feet. But now, if our factory produced shoes locally, there would be an alternative.

For years, our products had fulfilled wants, a luxury for a global audience that we were proud to export. But school shoes fulfilled a *need*, a solution for the everyday struggles of those in Haiti. I was convinced we had to adapt our business model and start producing school shoes as well.

Making school shoes and selling them to the organizations that cared deeply about educating Haiti's children was also a way to share our views about purchasing locally with people who had financial capacity and wanted to help Haiti succeed. I truly didn't think there was a better way to enhance our business than this.

Not everyone shared my conviction right away, however. Our stakeholders were skeptical, questioning whether this shift would dilute the luxury brand we had worked so hard to build. Including school shoes felt like a detour, a risk that might take us off course. But as I related parents' stories and explained the stakes, my conviction became contagious, and everyone got on board. This wasn't just a business decision; it was a mission. That's when Erony stepped forward. A skilled shoemaker with years of experience and an unshakable commitment to his craft, Erony became the heartbeat of this new vision. His expertise and leadership made it possible to turn an idea into a reality. We decided to disrupt our production line, take the leap, and begin with two bold initiatives at once: to redesign our luxury handbag line, and to manufacture durable, affordable leather school shoes for Haiti's children. It proved to be the right move at the right time. As one team of artisans mastered the intricate weaving of leather for our new handbag collections, under Erony's supervision, another was hard at work learning the art of making school shoes.

Meanwhile, the stateside team was eager to distribute the new woven handbag collections to the US market, but building a reputation as a trusted, sustainable luxury brand in this fiercely competitive market would take years we didn't have.

Time and money were luxuries we couldn't afford to gamble with. School shoes were different. They didn't require a long runway to success. From the moment we started production, the demand was there. Years of working in Haiti had built us a reputation of trust, both with the Haitian people and with the organizations that fund school programs for children. Now we were offering them something they desperately needed.

The organizations sponsoring students understood the pain point better than anyone, and we knew they would see the value in what we were offering. When we began this new venture our shoes sales were small, but they were constant. However, we needed something extraordinary to happen to fulfill the mission we had put before ourselves. And after about a year of courting, we found the perfect partner in an organization called Mission-Haiti. Its leadership team, led by husband and wife Paul and Bethany, shared our vision for economic freedom and justice in Haiti. They saw and understood the long-term impact of buying shoes for their 3,000 students directly from a Haitian shoe company. They became our first large-scale clients, and more than that, they became our greatest advocates in this endeavor.

Paul and Bethany used their platform to spread the word and convince their donors to forgo the shoe drive they orchestrated every year and purchase brand-new leather school shoes from Deux Mains instead. At its annual banquet, we were invited to speak and share intimately how the ripple effects of choosing to invest locally, to empower Haitian businesses, and to stimulate economic growth affect families in Haiti. Mission-Haiti wasn't just making a

Mission-Haiti students walking to school in their new shoes made at Deux Mains.

purchase; by choosing to disrupt a well-known charity endeavor like the annual shoe drive, it was making a statement. Its involvement became a turning point, proving that missions could be powerful agents of change, not only by providing immediate relief but by shaping a future in which Haiti could thrive on its own terms. With its support, we had made a real, tangible difference, not just for 3,000 students but for the future of our business.

It was almost surreal to see orders of such significance rolling in, especially during one of the most turbulent periods Haiti had faced in years. Our factory, although it had grown thanks to help from USAID and other investments, was still modest in size. But there was still room to press forward, while also protecting what we had built. With the environment still rife with political instability, we continued to tread carefully. Over the years we had watched as others, far better funded than we were, come and go. Developers with deep pockets, missions with lofty goals, and even celebrities with star power behind their ventures all tried to make a difference in Haiti, and most had failed. Factories backed by millions of dollars in investment would open with great fanfare, only to crumble under the immense pressure of doing business in this environment. Some didn't even last a year. However, the team, Sarah, and I poured every ounce of strength and attention we had into perfecting our school shoe operation. Then in an instant, our world changed.

It was Monday, and we just spent another long and exhausting shift at the factory. The day had stretched far beyond the hours we had promised ourselves we would work, but with the school year quickly approaching, every minute mattered. We needed to ensure that thousands of children would have shoes in time for their first day, and we needed to prove to ourselves that we could do it. In post-pandemic Haiti, still reeling from the assassination of the president, even small victories were a big deal.

Whatever the time of year, the heat always seemed relentless. We left the factory wearily, glad to be having dinner at the house of a friend, a frill we rarely allowed ourselves in these unstable days. Taylor was not only a great chef planning an exquisite dinner, but she also had a swimming pool, where we could relax and wash away the dust and unease of the day. The thought of the cool water was irresistible, and Sarah decided to take a quick dip before dinner. While the rest of us gathered around the table nibbling on snacks and chatting, she jumped into the water. I heard the splash but paid it no mind, assuming Sarah was enjoying the pool. A moment later I glanced over and saw her face down, her limp body floating to the surface. For a split second, I thought she was joking. Sarah had always been a bit of a prankster, so I called out, "Stop messing around!" But before I could finish the sentence, our friend Jordany had raced to the pool and leaped in. He pulled her limp body upright out of the water, and Sarah's face, contorted by pure fear and horror, was all I could see.

It was dark and she had misjudged the pool's depth, colliding with the concrete floor. I jumped in, and when I reached her, she looked at me with wide eyes. "Jules, I can't feel my legs."

Her words punched me in the chest, and I immediately grabbed her neck with both hands. Within seconds, the others were kneeling by the edge of the pool ready to help Jordany and me to pull her out of the water. Taylor was quick to call HERO, one of the only working ambulance and emergency services in Haiti. Time seemed to stop; I can't remember whether it took minutes or hours for them to arrive. I recall only the unbearable waiting and the feeling of blood trickling down my fingers as I cupped my hands tightly around Sarah's neck, refusing to let go.

When the HERO team arrived, one of the responders gently placed a hand on mine. "You need to let go," he said softly, his calm demeanor a stark contrast to the chaos around us. I refused, terrified that even the smallest movement might make things worse. He gently moved my hands, replacing them with an old-fashioned neck brace. He was confident as he placed Sarah on a backboard and lifted her into the ambulance. I looked down at the blood on my fingers. Still wet, I climbed into the back of the ambulance. The gang activity around the hospital didn't cross my mind, but HERO's manager Stacy was all too familiar with the risks. She insisted on an armored escort, complete with a low-profile vehicle and a two-man security team armed with long guns. The dramatic rescue and harrowing ambulance ride to the hospital were just the beginning of a very long thirty-six-hour ordeal to get Sarah out of Haiti.

The emergency room at Clinique Lambert Santé in Pétion-Ville was stark, and the hospital ill-equipped for the gravity of Sarah's condition. The staff worked diligently but were clearly constrained by a lack of resources. Without an x-ray machine or any sort of equipment to conduct a proper diagnosis, their faces were grave, their solemnity a reflection of the dire situation. Sarah lay completely still, her arms totally unresponsive. She was dressed in a torn hospital gown, and the neck brace, straight out of the 1960s, clung awkwardly to her face. At the time, however, we had no idea this relic was the only thing keeping her fractured spinal cord intact. Conversations with the surgeon and doctor went in circles; their hands were tied by the hospital's limitations. It was clear that Sarah couldn't stay there, not if she were to have any chance of using her limbs again. She needed to get to the United States, to a hospital with the expertise and equipment to handle her injuries. I made several phone calls, my voice strained with urgency and desperate for help, but to no avail. And then things became very still.

Even with medical evacuation and insurance paperwork in my hand, this was a task I wasn't remotely prepared to handle. Stacy became my lifeline. She patiently walked me step by step through the process we needed to get Sarah out of Haiti and to a US hospital where she could be properly treated. The first hurdle was to arrange a medical evacuation plane, a feat that seemed impossible given the situation on the ground. Landing a plane in Haiti in the middle of the night was risky enough, but doing so in gang-controlled territory entailed an entirely new level of danger. We had to pay $24,000 up front to secure the plane before any other action could take place. Sarah's condition didn't matter to anyone I spoke to; nothing could move forward without our first covering that amount. I scrambled to pull the funds together, all the while fighting back the creeping fear that we might not make it in time.

After a few hours, the plane was secured. We next needed to find a hospital that would accept Sarah's US medical insurance. From the start, we met resistance. It was an impossible puzzle, each step dependent on another, but each fraught with delays and complications. Meanwhile, Sarah lay motionless in that stark hospital room, her fate hanging in the balance. Stacy and her team worked continuously, navigating a labyrinth of logistics. After paying the $24,000 to the plane company and securing a pick-up time, we hit a devastating roadblock. We couldn't find a hospital in Florida willing to take a spinal cord injury patient from Haiti. Without a hospital to receive us, we were trapped.

For nine grueling hours hospital after hospital turned us down, but Stacy was unrelenting. Finally she was able to secure treatment for Sarah at St. Mary's Hospital in West Palm Beach, Florida. Relief washed over me, but it was short-lived. By the time the arrangements were finalized, our original flight had been cancelled due to the delay. Then we were informed that securing a new medical evacuation flight and team would require an entirely new payment upfront. It would take three days to process the refund of the first flight's down payment, leaving us with no immediate access to the $24,000 we had scraped together. Sarah's family and I had already maxed out our credit cards, and we didn't have credit available to secure a second plane.

I paced the halls of the empty hospital, unable to think straight. Every second that passed felt like another step closer to losing Sarah. In a panic I called Stacy and left her a voicemail, my voice shaking as I explained the situation. "I don't know what to do," I said, the words heavy with fear and exhaustion.

Minutes later my phone buzzed with a life-changing text. I had to read it three times to process it. Stacy had written,

"Julie, I'll put the $24,000 down payment on my card, and you can pay me back when you are reimbursed by the first company."

"WHAT???" I frantically typed back. Her generosity was staggering.

Stacy and I had known each other since 2010, when the earthquake had brought countless aid workers to the country. Our paths had crossed many times in those early days, but over the years our lives had drifted into different orbits, hers with HERO and mine with REBUILD globally and Deux Mains. Her response came quickly.

"Back in 2010, you gave me food and water and I never forgot. Favor repaid! ☺" I couldn't remember what she was talking about. But the fact that she remembered a small thing I had done a decade ago left me breathless. Words failed me. All I could do was whisper a silent prayer of thanks and focus on the next step: getting Sarah to safety.

I sat on the bed across from Sarah. My still-damp clothes clung to me but I barely noticed. I watched Sarah's long eyelashes flutter as her eyes opened and closed. It was the only way I knew she was still alive. In all my years in Haiti, I had never had to make the kind of call I made that night, to tell someone's mother that her child had been in a terrible accident. My heart ached at the tremor in Sarah's mother's voice, asking questions I couldn't answer. And in all my life, I have never been so terrified that someone I love so deeply might never walk or use their arms again.

It was a long night of organizing next steps and balancing an array of emotions, waiting to be evacuated. Thirty-six hours later we boarded a small medical plane with a doctor and a nurse escorting us back to the United States. As she lay on the gurney in her inadequate neck brace, Sarah stared straight into my eyes.

"Promise me," she said, her voice barely above a whisper, "that nothing bad will happen to Deux Mains because of this." How could I promise that, when I couldn't even fathom what the company, or my life, would look like without her? But I nodded, swallowing the lump in my throat.

"I promise," I whispered back.

A few hours later, surgeons pieced Sarah's vertebrae back together, giving her a chance to regain mobility. Life at St. Mary's Hospital became our new normal. Deux Mains and REBUILD kept us both anchored during that time. My promise that our organization would be okay gave Sarah a purpose to fight for and me a mission to cling to during the months of uncertainty that followed. Eventually Sarah inched her way back to health, gaining strength and learning to use her hands and body again. And in time she made a miraculous recovery, one that continues to stump every doctor we see. Although her body healed in an incredible way, the nerve damage from the accident will continue to be a long battle, yet never has her dedication to our work in Haiti faltered. Her resilience, matched with a positivity and determination I've never seen in anyone else, became the foundation of her recovery.

During those months as I sat by Sarah's side, the young leadership team at the factory stepped up in ways that left me in awe. With tenacity and minimal guidance they carried out the new school shoe project, navigating challenges with the confidence of seasoned professionals. Watching them from a distance was both humbling and inspiring. These

Spring 2013 and 2024, Port-au-Prince, Haiti. This is Rony when he started in the REBUILD globally education program, and after his transformation and growth as the Operations Manager at Deux Mains. He is the epitome of what is possible when opportunities for education and work are available.

were young graduates of our charity program, thrust into a world of fashion management with little preparation but proving their fortitude time and again.

Lovely and Rony emerged as leaders during this period. With the support of the rest of the team, they began to manage all production and Haiti operations in the factory. Lovely, always steady and organized, took charge of the administration of the factory. Rony, who had been Sarah's executive assistant and trusted right hand, took on managing all Haiti operations. The day after Sarah's surgery, with eyes welling up, he told me not to worry about anything. "God will help me take on all of Sarah's duties," he said with confident determination. Payroll was the most intricate of these duties. It included managing employee bonuses and calculating the match amount for our university scholarship program, a task Sarah had always approached with meticulous care. Rony knew it would be complicated, but "I will take my laptop home and learn how to do it," he assured me.

His voice was resolute as he added, "One day, I will become Sarah. I will make her proud of me and do everything in my power to keep the factory open." Rony did far more than anyone could have expected. He inspired the entire team at the factory to come together to ensure the survival of our shared dream. Their leadership gave us the strength to overcome another tragedy in our young but turbulent life as a family.

CHAPTER 17

THE SOUL OF MONEY

> Whether we look at money in the context of our personal or family lives, the workplace, or in the health and welfare of nations, the same picture emerges: Money is the most universally motivating, mischievous, miraculous, maligned and misunderstood part of contemporary life.
>
> *Lynne Twist*

○

Fifteen years. That's how long it's taken me to finish this book. As therapeutic as writing it has been, sometimes the memories came too fast and too raw, cutting deep. Other times they felt like ghosts slipping through my fingers before I could capture them. Writing about Haiti, about all the heartbreak and hope, was like tending a garden of memories. Some bloomed brilliantly, while others paralyzed me with the fear that I couldn't do our story justice. I always wanted to find the right words to make someone feel the way I did in those moments, to understand the heat of the factory, the desperation of a hospital without supplies, or the joy of seeing a child walk to school in a pair of shoes we had made.

But was it even possible to express all that Haiti has taught me, all it has given and taken away?

As I ventured down this path of frantic scribbling and annoying writer's block, I'd remind myself why I was writing this story in the first place. Books have the power to change lives in the most significant ways. It is my greatest hope that our story of Haiti, our journey of friendship, love, loss, and business-building, will matter to someone else in the same way a book changed my life many years ago. I was in my late twenties when I read *The Soul of Money* by Lynne Twist and started to unravel what money meant, not as a measure of wealth but as a measure of freedom. Thus the title of this last chapter of my story is a tribute to her book and to her.

Twist's book opened my eyes to the greatness of a single dollar, not in its power to accumulate, but in its ability to create opportunity in the developing world. As I traced back some of the generous dollars we received as charitable gifts to REBUILD globally, or the profit from products sold at Deux Mains, I found myself captivated by their impact. Hearing stories from the people who received these dollars as they reminisced about how they spent or saved them often left me awestruck, just as our customers and donors did when they recalled what their purchases and/or investments meant to them. These interactions were often powerful reminders that even the smallest gestures could ripple outward in unimaginable ways.

In 2011, Jim and Mark had been sent by my alma mater, the University of Central Florida (UCF), to record our work in the form of a short video to present at UCF's annual

Black and Gold Gala, where I would be honored with the Alumni Association's Community Service Award. Even a year after the disaster, the two were greeted by the still-shattered remains of an airport that seemed on the verge of collapse. Haitian airline employees struggled to enforce any semblance of order as passengers debarked, but the effort was futile. Jim's senses were overloaded as swarms of insects attacked his bare skin and dozens of Haitian men scrambled to his side, jostling for the chance to carry his bags in exchange for a few precious coins. When I met them at the airport exit, their faces showed a mix of curiosity, discomfort, and disbelief, emotions familiar to anyone stepping into the raw intensity of Haiti for the first time. It was a scorching week in August, but Jim and Mark were carrying cameras and a mission, and they tried hard to ignore the conditions.

While I was pleased to be recognized with this award, what was even more powerful was the chance to tell the story of REBUILD globally and Deux Mains to a wider audience at the gala. As professional storytellers, Mark and Jim immersed themselves in the rhythm of our world, capturing pieces of our chaotic and beautiful life in Haiti, seeking to weave a narrative that could bridge the gap between our work and the people who would be eager to understand what we were doing. Their cameras focused on the bustling energy of our workshop and the students back in classrooms. When they finally returned to the United States, they carried a raw and honest video that distilled the essence of our work, a reflection of the legacy we were building in a place so often defined by loss.

The night of the gala I stood on stage, the Community Service Award in my hand, with Mark and Jim's video playing for a room full of influential alumni and Orlando locals. The images on the screen transported the audience to Haiti, to our workshop where hands were crafting with pride and purpose, to young students in our outdoor tutoring center eager to learn new lessons, to the rivers of trash that overflowed in the streets. The contrast screamed from the screen. The room was silent, captivated not just by the visuals but by the tale they told. The impact of REBUILD globally and Deux Mains reached hearts far beyond our small community that night, and the narrative of despair once splashed across CNN in the wake of the earthquake was now replaced by a story of strong, proud Haitian people reclaiming their lives, rebuilding their homes, and reigniting their communities.

The gala was one of those rare events that leaves everyone feeling hopeful, connected, and ready to change the world. For most, that feeling fades with the last sip of champagne. But for Jim it didn't. Every year since his initial trip, he has volunteered his time and his team to return to the island, capturing the growth of REBUILD globally and Deux Mains, carefully balancing honesty with hope, and ensuring that the starkness of poverty never overshadows the weight of our work.

Jim's words, photos, and videos inspired many people over the years through fundraisers, art shows, and exhibitions. But perhaps one of the biggest impressions he left was on his wife, Beth. For years, Beth supported Jim as he spent time in Haiti capturing stories and weeks back home editing them. She encouraged his passion, giving him the freedom to immerse himself in the work that mattered most to him. Yet it wasn't until 2017 that she took the flight across the Caribbean to see Haiti for herself, and it didn't take long for Haiti to enchant her and capture her entrepreneurial spirit. The importance of creating jobs resonated deeply with her and she wanted to be a part of this movement.

Back in Orlando, Beth is one of the city's most successful realtors. For years, part of her signature service was a personalized gift basket full of practical items that her team prepared for every buyer's first night in a new home. After her time in Haiti, Beth began to see these gestures differently—the plastic baskets were disposable and wasteful, made without giving any thought to ethical production or sustainability. Beth realized these gifts, intended to celebrate a new beginning, were contributing to the very cycle of mass production and waste she now wanted to help change.

Inspired by her experience at Deux Mains, Beth decided to reimagine her business practice to make a greater impact. She worked with the talented artisans in Haiti and a local Orlando artist to design a beautiful custom bag to replace the baskets. The Beth Bag, as it is called in Haiti, isn't just a gesture; it's a way to do business better. It is an order we can count on every year at Deux Mains, a steady source of work, and the ripple effect is profound. The power of a dollar—one dollar, strategically placed—became a hundred, a thousand. Like Jim, Beth was determined to use her business and talents as a force for good, and she led by example to inspire other businesses to do the same.

Before the earthquake, understanding Haiti's complexities wasn't a priority for me, nor was understanding the power of business. However, after I thrust myself into the complicated scenarios of the Haitian recovery efforts, I was faced with the reality that charity and international development, even well-funded efforts, can sometimes be ineffective or even harmful. Engulfed by the intricacies of the cycle of aid, I experienced firsthand that charitable gifts and donations are vital but can easily be misused. Aid dollars must be delivered with an understanding of the broader context and used as more than just a temporary fix. With the incredible power these dollars hold, they should aim to empower sustainably, not just alleviate immediate suffering.

Long before the earthquake, Haiti was already saturated with charitable efforts. About 10,000 NGOs operated in the country, more per capita than in any other country in the world, earning it the nickname "the Republic of NGOs." Yet despite this massive influx of aid, Haiti still suffers from extreme poverty. If nonprofits and aid alone were truly the solution, why hadn't things changed? Jonathan Katz, the only full-time foreign correspondent in Haiti at the time of the earthquake, paints a sobering picture in his book *The Big Truck That Went By: How the World Came to Save Haiti and Left Behind a Disaster*. Katz tells how UN troops inadvertently brought cholera to a country where it had not existed, how millions of dollars raised for relief efforts were misused by organizations like the American Red Cross, and how aid workers from outside Haiti operated without any real oversight or accountability. His accounts weren't just statistics or headlines; they were the reality of a country deeply affected by well-meaning but flawed efforts. It was through witnessing these frustrating truths that I began to understand the system was set up to keep people stuck in poverty, rather than empowering them to create their own opportunities.

As someone keenly aware of the unintended harm caused by many nonprofits, I understand the great irony of creating yet another one. But REBUILD globally was never born from charity; it was born from conviction. Years of witnessing broken systems taught me that true sustainability means people must have the power to shape their own futures. That's why REBUILD globally and Deux Mains are forever intertwined—one prepares people for work, and the other provides it. Together, they form a living cycle of empowerment.

Guided by the lessons in *The Soul of Money*, we set out to ensure every dollar created a ripple effect—reaching farther, touching more lives, and multiplying its impact long after its first use. That vision demanded more than good intentions; it required authentic relationships. Some of our most transformative initiatives began not in boardrooms, but under mango trees and around shared meals, where trust and shared purpose turned simple conversations into partnerships that changed lives for years to come.

As I reflect more about *The Soul Of Money*, it reminds me of several serendipitous moments that have changed the course of our charity and business.

After a few demanding years in Haiti, Billy and I were thrilled to get away for a friend's wedding in Las Vegas. We had big plans to dance the night away with people I hadn't seen in far too long and spend our days enjoying the freedom of hiking the Grand Canyon. But as our plane descended into the glittering city, a sense of discomfort gnawed at me.

We had been living in a place where the simplest things, like electricity, were luxuries for so many, and now we were heading to the very city where excess was the norm. I was having an existential crisis about it. I felt an overwhelming anxiety, and instead of taking deep breaths or silently sitting in my seat, I leaned forward, almost falling into the man beside me as I stared out the window. I half-expected the man to nudge me, tell me to stop leaning into his space. But instead he smiled and spoke gently, his voice cutting through my restless thoughts.

"Hi, I'm Scott. Is this your first time on an airplane?"

His question, simple as it was, caught me off guard. This was probably my hundredth flight, but I realized my actions must have indicated I was a novice traveler, and being so wrapped up in my own feelings, I hadn't even noticed I was invading his personal space. I apologized, but Scott just shrugged it off.

"It's okay," he said. "I can tell you've got a lot on your mind."

Grateful for his warm smile, I laughed and responded, "No, this isn't my first flight, but it's my first time out of Haiti in a few months." Intrigued that I was coming from Haiti, Scott started to ask lots of questions, and I happily related the challenges of having a charity and a business in Haiti.

I was particularly concerned with a young woman in the REBUILD globally program. She was a great student with so much potential, but lately she had become solemn and quiet. I didn't know how to help her, and it was weighing heavily on me.

To my surprise, Scott didn't seem bothered by the intensity of my words. In fact, he leaned in, interested, engaged. He listened intently and then proceeded to tell Billy and me about his life, business, and family. Scott, it turned out, wasn't just some random seatmate. In the middle of what could have been an ordinary flight, a relationship began that has deepened over a decade. By the time we landed in Vegas, Scott had decided he would tithe ten percent of his earnings to sustain the education program at REBUILD globally.

Since that flight to Las Vegas, my life has been intertwined with those of Scott and his wife Donna, who are regular supporters of Haiti. To this day, I can't quite pinpoint how or why certain people have come into our community, but I know one thing for sure: This is the kind of generosity that propels REBUILD globally to continue ensuring young people graduate high school well prepared for college or a career.

Sarah had a similarly impactful encounter years later when she first moved to Haiti to work with me and made a connection that would also help define our ability to sustainably operate REBUILD globally. She made plans to meet a friend at a small café for lunch. As they chatted, the door swung open and in walked Joan, a woman with a heart full of purpose and a deep love for Haiti. Joan was accompanied by her niece Tiffany, a young woman studying social work who had recently moved to Haiti to join her aunt's efforts. As they walked by Sarah's table, Tiffany noticed they were about the same age and struck up a conversation.

Moments later the women pulled up chairs to join Sarah's table. Sarah learned that Joan's connection to Haiti ran deep. She had been in the country during the 2010 earthquake and checked out of the Montana Hotel the same day the building had collapsed, burying fifty-two victims in rubble. Her miraculous escape left Joan with a profound bond to the people of Haiti and a fierce determination to make a difference. Her heart especially ached for the *restavek* children, abandoned by parents who lack resources and forced into servitude. Unable to shake the thought of them and feeling God leading her to take action, she founded Restavek Freedom, an organization aimed at rescuing these children from abuse and offering them a path to freedom.

The group talked for hours, conversation flowing naturally as they each shared their visions for their organizations. Joan was intrigued by the work we were doing at REBUILD globally and Deux Mains. Like most others, she had never heard of a model quite like ours. A few days later Joan and Tiffany made the trek down to Tabarre to visit our operation in person. They were impressed with what they witnessed, and Joan saw an opportunity. She had an ability to connect people in meaningful ways, and after seeing our work firsthand, she looked at Sarah with a knowing smile and said, "I need you to meet my good friend Jeanie."

When Jeanie visited Haiti a short time later, Joan made sure to bring her to the workshop. Just as she had predicted, Jeanie was immediately struck by the impact we were having in Haiti. I was in the United States at the time of Jeanie's visit, but Sarah thought it was essential that we meet in person. She tried to arrange a time when both Jeanie and I would be in Haiti next, but Jeanie had another plan. Instead of waiting for the right time in Haiti, she said, "Have Julie come to my home in Pennsylvania."

A few weeks later I found myself nervously driving into a small, quiet town in northern Pennsylvania. I didn't know exactly what to expect from the woman I was about to meet, but I had heard enough about Jeanie to know that she was someone with a heart full of compassion and a deep commitment to support work she felt aligned to. Her family had been longtime supporters of missions around the world, pouring resources and energy into communities far and wide.

Jeanie met me with a warm, welcoming smile and suggested we walk to a local park. After my long morning of travel, I was grateful to stretch my legs. She led me up the road to a peaceful playground with lots of greenery, and we sat at a picnic bench near a pond. The quiet rustle of leaves seemed to set the tone as I started to describe my big dreams for the students at REBUILD globally, hoping to convey the urgency of our work and the vision I carried for the future. Jeanie listened intently, her eyes never leaving mine, and I could see that she wasn't just hearing my words, she was absorbing them, understanding the depth of what we were trying to do.

Reciprocating, Jeanie told me stories about her dedication to working in the developing world, and the projects in which she had been active over the years. Though our programs were different, I could sense a kindred spirit. Jeanie's faith was unshakeable, a fierce, quiet strength that let me know she trusted her gut. She was drawn to what we were doing in Haiti, not because it fit neatly into any formula, but because it was rooted in faith, love, and a deep desire to see change.

In the months that followed, Jeanie unexpectedly became one of our most trusted allies. With her knowledge of development and holistic programming, she offered ideas on ways we could refine our students' curriculum. As she continued to work with us, it was easy to see that her investments in the students would be significant, but what surprised me was the way she became a steady source of strength for me personally, especially when my faith was being challenged. Jeanie was always available to support me, to lift us back up, and to offer a new path forward. Her love for people and her capacity to bestow so much financially, spiritually, and emotionally continues to enhance our work at REBUILD globally.

As our time in Haiti continues, the present-day situation constantly introduces new challenges for us, and the need to create more jobs has dramatically increased. Many ateliers and factories have succumbed in gang-infested areas, forced to close their doors. The voices of workers displaced by these closures tell the same story that they did fifteen years ago: the longing for a good job and a consistent paycheck, ensuring there is money to feed their children and make payments towards their education, all still necessities during these turbulent times. As one of the only factories still operational in Port-au-Prince, we remain steadfast in our determination to stay open, but once again, we couldn't face this growing need alone.

Scaling our impact demanded more than our loyal investors, dedicated artisans, and even our existing customer base. To employ more craftspeople safely and efficiently, we needed to forge connections with clients capable of making substantial and consistent purchases. Among our supporters at REBUILD globally, many were profoundly touched by the transformation happening at Deux Mains, Jeanie in particular. She remembers her visit to the new factory and the way the pride that radiated from the room stirred something fundamental within her. Jeanie was realizing that the economic development of Haiti would require not just education but also opportunities for sustainable work.

Over the past few years she has turned this realization into revolutionary action and become a leader in the movement among other missions and nonprofit organizations in Haiti to buy locally. Jeanie first changed her own buying habits and started purchasing what she could directly from Haitian businesses rather than importing it. Soon she became another one of our biggest clients at Deux Mains, purchasing thousands of sandals for the women in a maternity clinic she supported, and thousands of school shoes for the children in schools she worked with. She introduced us to international clients with whom she had influence so they could also contract for thousands of our bags and accessories. Her advocacy to other NGOs and missions to buy Haitian-made goods has been a beacon to inspire them to invest in that purpose and create long-term support for our business.

Fighting for every dollar we earned through the sale of our products was never just our goal, but the foundation of our legacy. We became a living example that every purchase has the power to change lives and create opportunity where it is most needed. There is a responsible way to build the economy, and it starts with each one of us. Every day we all make choices about what we buy, from the food we eat, to the clothes we wear, to the little luxuries we allow ourselves. What we buy may seem like a personal decision, but each purchase has far-reaching effects, and that gives us a lot of power to shape the world around us. It inspires me to know the power to create good jobs lies in our hands.

What we have built in Haiti is a combination of efforts made by the people who have stood beside us, whether through a contribution or a purchase from Deux Mains, and by those of us who have physically labored to create our company. However, I believe our greatest triumph is less about what we built, and more about who we became. What sets us apart now, and what fills me with the deepest pride, is that we are Haitian-operated and Haitian-managed. It was my dream to ensure that the people of Haiti were not just part of the process but were the ones driving it. Today, that dream has come to life. The very students who once walked through REBUILD's doors are now leading Deux Mains into the future. The reins are in their hands, exactly where they belong.

Lovely once told me that even though we don't share a last name or a nationality, the work family we've built has made her a stronger woman. Even in the years I couldn't travel to Haiti because of the violence, the foundation we laid empowered the team to lead and thrive. She believes that made all the difference when it was us against the world, which seems to be often these days. Her words echoed what I always felt: the strongest parts of me were shaped in Haiti, molded by the quiet courage and fierce determination of this team. But it was under the leadership of Lovely, Rony, and Jolina that we didn't just challenge the systems of inequality built on poverty and exploitation; we replaced them. We built something better, even pushing ourselves to go through the rigorous process to become verified by the Fair Trade Federation, a badge of honor that affirms our commitment to dignity, justice, and sustainable development. It wasn't easy, but it was worth every form, every standard, every hour. Because it meant our entire factory, every product, and every person behind it, is part of something greater than ourselves. It meant we could look the world in the eye and say, *We are proof that another way is possible.*

We fully invested in the young people who walked through our doors so many years ago, and now we get to stand back and watch as miracles unfold. I imagine this is what it must feel like to be a proud parent, witnessing your children flourish against all odds. Although the ache of not being a traditional mother still lives deep in my soul, I have been given the gift of being the matriarch of this family, this extraordinary, resilient family, one born not of blood, but of purpose. This gift has allowed me to bear witness to people who stared down loss time and time again and said, "Not today. Not us." It is a family whose quiet courage has transformed mere survival into a legacy, whose refusal to be defined by calamity has created a resolute passion for change. And as we look to the future, we do so with unwavering love and an unshakable will, because together we are not just dreaming the impossible. We are living it.

Shop Deux Mains and help us change the world, one bag at a time.

ACKNOWLEDGMENTS

It has now been a decade and a half since I left my job and home in Florida to become immersed in a new culture, where I ungracefully butchered the Creole language, battled an array of rashes and stomach illnesses, founded an international charity, and became the president of an ethical fashion business. This was an industry foreign to me, but I did it to launch a model for creating a social business to fight poverty sustainably. I have lived more in these years than in all my others combined, and I am forever indebted to the courageous people of Haiti, my husband, family, friends, colleagues, volunteers, interns, and other agencies in Haiti and the United States that have made REBUILD globally and Deux Mains a reality.

Thank you to each one of you who never gave up, even when it felt like there was nothing left to hold on to. Your hope and belief in dignified job creation gave us the strongest army on the battlefield. As our fashion business evolved and developed over the years, the circumstances of my life changed dramatically as well. The only consistent notion that remained was that this book had to be written. I would like to give my utmost thanks to my team, who have shared their memories with me and pushed me to finish telling our story. However, thanks do not begin to cover the gratitude I feel for your making my life so worthwhile.

We wanted the significant lessons we learned in our fight against economic injustice to be shared in the hope it could support others as they live out their calling to make the world a more just and sustainable place. Despite Haiti's difficult history, Haitians have a way of giving hope to others, and their experiences should not be forgotten. Even though I am sure I will never fully understand their countless stories, I know they greatly influenced mine.

ABOUT THE AUTHOR

Julie Colombino-Billingham, former aid worker and native of Florida, is the founder of Deux Mains, a global fair-trade fashion business in Haiti that uses the native wisdom of its people to create jobs. Inspired to find a better way to help disaster victims recover their livelihoods and their dignity, Colombino-Billingham flew to Haiti following the devastating earthquake of 2010 and stayed for years, falling in love with the Haitian people, their strength, and their resourcefulness.

She was a top 25 finalist for the 2025 WE Empower UN SDG Challenge, and the 2018 recipient of the Southern Living Beauty Awards for her work as a female entrepreneur. A finalist for the 2017 Digicel Entrepreneur of the Year Award in Haiti and the 2016 Martin Bell Scholar, she recently received her MBA from Rollins Crummer Graduate School of Business. *From Loss to Legacy* is her riveting memoir of her work in Haiti, and her account of the revolutionary approach to disaster aid that she developed there.

ABOUT BOLD STORY PRESS

Bold Story Press is a curated, woman-owned hybrid publishing company with a mission of publishing well-written stories by women. If your book is chosen for publication, our team of expert editors and designers will work with you to publish a professionally edited and designed book. Every woman has a story to tell. If you have written yours and want to explore publishing with Bold Story Press, contact us at https://boldstorypress.com.

The Bold Story Press logo, designed by Grace Arsenault, was inspired by the nom de plume, or pen name, a sad necessity at one time for female authors who wanted to publish. The woman's face hidden in the quill is the profile of Virginia Woolf, who, in addition to being an early feminist writer, founded and ran her own publishing company, Hogarth Press.

Thank you for reading our story.

If you enjoyed it, please tell a friend and consider leaving a review on Amazon or Goodreads— it makes a huge impact.

www.ingramcontent.com/pod-product-compliance
Lightning Source LLC
Chambersburg PA
CBHW020149090426
42734CB00008B/750